An Incremental Writing Program

Primary Book A
Teacher's Guide

Nancy I. Sanders

WriteShop Primary Book A Teacher's Guide

© 2008 by Nancy I. Sanders.

Published and distributed by Demme Learning

All rights reserved. No part of this book may be reproduced, stored in a retrieval system, or transmitted in any form by any means—electronic, mechanical, photocopying, recording, or otherwise—without prior written permission from Demme Learning.

The use or mention of a supplemental resource does not imply endorsement by the author and publisher, nor does it imply that said resource endorses this book.

This book contains a variety of projects that complement the WriteShop curriculum. Instructors should carefully supervise and assist students with all projects. Projects are undertaken at the user's sole risk.

The author and publisher specifically disclaim all responsibility and accept no liability for any loss, injury or risk, personal or otherwise, resulting from or arising out of the use and application of this book and its contents, including without limitation projects and resources mentioned herein.

Please note that online resources that were available at the time of publishing may have been updated or may no longer be available.

writeshop.com

1-888-854-6284 or +1 717-283-1448 | demmelearning.com
Lancaster, Pennsylvania USA

ISBN 978-1-935027-00-3
Revision Code 0108

Printed in the United States of America by The P.A. Hutchison Company
2 3 4 5 6 7 8 9 10

For information regarding CPSIA on this printed material call: 1-888-854-6284
and provide reference #0108-01142022

Dedication

To my mother, Phyllis Hershberger, who taught me to love to read and inspired me to write.

Table of Contents

Welcome and Introduction

Welcome to WriteShop Primary

Learning to write is an exciting adventure for both you and your child. Welcome to WriteShop Primary, where the creative journey begins!

Understanding the Purpose of WriteShop Primary

Developed for students in grades K-3, WriteShop Primary is designed for parents to work closely with their young children. As you interact with your child, you help him explore the world of words through a variety of colorful and meaningful activities.

WriteShop Primary is not meant to be a rigorous writing program. It is an introduction to early writing skills that gives young children tools to experience success as they develop the ability to write. Whether you have a more advanced child or one who is just beginning, this program is flexible so students can work at their own level.

Each WriteShop Primary book can be used independently, but the incremental nature of the program encourages you to take your child through all three levels: Book A, Book B, and Book C. Although the parent of a more advanced child may decide to skip Book A and jump right into Book B or C, most find value in starting at the beginning. Starting your child in Book A will ensure that he understands the basics. Even as you review foundational concepts with your child, you can simultaneously keep him challenged with the advanced-level activities suggested in the Flying Higher and Want to Do More? activities you will see throughout the curriculum.

Above all, we want you to have fun! Your zeal and encouragement will bring joy to your child's journey as she learns that writing can be a pleasure rather than a chore.

Teaching Young Children to Write

Children develop at different rates. Fine-motor skills, like other stages of development, vary from child to child. Some budding writers, especially boys, will struggle with writing on a line, copying and forming letters, and putting their words and thoughts on paper. These skills and more come with time and patience.

The development of a young child's writing is best achieved through:

- Plenty of time spent on writing activities.
- Many opportunities to write during the school day.
- Focused instruction that builds from your child's efforts.

Clearly, young children cannot learn to write on their own. Even if you create an atmosphere rich with educational materials—picture books, lined paper, colored markers, crayons, and an alphabet chart—it's not enough. To effectively develop basic writing skills, your child needs YOU—along with your example, encouragement, and daily guidance.

This season in your child's educational development is an opportune time to teach and model writing within a warm, safe environment. As you progress through WriteShop Primary lessons, you'll soon find that repetition, routine, and consistency play a vital role in teaching basic skills. There's no way around it—your involvement with your child during writing sessions is key to his success!

Planning Your Schedule

Because WriteShop Primary is ungraded, your child may begin Book A any time between kindergarten and second grade. Book A is not recommended for third graders, as the projects and activities are geared toward younger children.

For this reason, you will find that the scheduling plans on pages 3-6 do not mention third graders. These older children, as well as most second graders, should begin WriteShop Primary in Book B or C.

Typically, if you begin Book A when your child is in:

- Kindergarten or first grade, you will
  - ~ Choose the Three-Week Lesson Plan
  - ~ Complete WriteShop Primary in three years
- First or second grade, you will
  - ~ Choose the Two-Week Lesson Plan
  - ~ Complete WriteShop Primary in two years
- Second grade, you will
  - ~ Choose the One-Week Lesson Plan
  - ~ Complete WriteShop Primary in one year

If you plan to start your second or third grader in Book B or C, you will find appropriate scheduling guidelines in each book.

	Kindergarten/First	First/Second Grade	Second Grade
Three-Week Lesson Plan (3 books in 3 years)	Book A	Book B	Book C
Two-Week Lesson Plan (3 books in 2 years)		Book A, Book B	Book B, Book C
One-Week Lesson Plan (3 books in 1 year)			A, B, C

Most children will fit nicely into one of these standard plans. However, a child who is delayed, reluctant, or advanced may need to work at a different pace. In that case, feel free to work at a faster or slower pace.

Choosing a Plan

The following overviews will explain each of the above three plans in order to help you choose the most appropriate schedule for your child.

Three-Week Lesson Plan

When beginning with Book A, this plan is ideal for a kindergartener or first grader.

Using this plan, you will:

- Do one lesson every three weeks, working three days per week.
- Complete all of WriteShop Primary in three years.
  - ~ Book A in 30 weeks (first year)
  - ~ Book B in 30 weeks (second year)
  - ~ Book C in 30 weeks (third year)

The Three-Week Plan is the slowest schedule, making it ideal for the younger or challenged student. This unhurried pace allows you to complete each lesson over three weeks with plenty of flexibility, reducing frustration and ensuring mastery. By following this schedule, you will work on WriteShop Primary three days a week. The schedule below shows a typical Monday-Friday school week, but you should feel free to choose the days of the week that work best for your family.

Spreading activities into "Off" days also allows more time to complete lessons that may be interrupted by holidays, field trips, or unexpected events.

The Three-Week Plan for one lesson looks like this:

Monday Activity Set 1	**Tuesday**	**Wednesday Activity Set 2**	**Thursday**	**Friday Activity Set 3**
Guided Writing Practice	Off	Guided Writing Practice Pre-writing Activities	Off	Guided Writing Practice Brainstorming

Monday Activity Set 4	**Tuesday**	**Wednesday Activity Set 5**	**Thursday**	**Friday Activity Set 6**
Guided Writing Practice The Writing Project	Off	Guided Writing Practice Editing and Revising	Off	Guided Writing Practice Activity Set Worksheet

Monday Activity Set 7	**Tuesday**	**Wednesday Activity Set 8**	**Thursday**	**Friday**
Guided Writing Practice Publishing the Writing Project	Off	Guided Writing Practice Evaluating Student's Work Want to Do More?	Off	Off

Two-Week Lesson Plan

When beginning with Book A, this plan is ideal for:

- A first grader.
- A second grader with limited writing experience.

Using this plan, you will:

- Do one lesson every two weeks, working four days per week.
- Complete all of WriteShop Primary in two years.
    - ~ Book A in 20 weeks
    - ~ Book B in 20 weeks
    - ~ Book C in 20 weeks

The Two-Week Lesson Plan sets a modest pace, making it ideal for a child with little or no writing experience. This is also a good schedule choice when working with multiple ages/ability levels at one time. If you are teaching children at different grade levels, challenge the older ones by expecting more from them and by doing the optional activities.

Using this plan, you will still follow the same order of Activity Sets as the Three-Week Lesson Plan. However, by eliminating the "Off" days found in the three-week schedule, you will finish each lesson in two weeks instead of three.

The Two-Week Lesson Plan for one lesson looks like this:

Monday Activity Set 1	**Tuesday Activity Set 2**	**Wednesday Activity Set 3**	**Thursday Activity Set 4**	**Friday**
Guided Writing Practice	Guided Writing Practice	Guided Writing Practice	Guided Writing Practice	Off
	Pre-writing Activities	Brainstorming	The Writing Project	

Monday Activity Set 5	**Tuesday Activity Set 6**	**Wednesday Activity Set 7**	**Thursday Activity Set 8**	**Friday**
Guided Writing Practice	Guided Writing Practice	Guided Writing Practice	Guided Writing Practice	Off
Editing and Revising	Activity Set Worksheet	Publishing the Project	Evaluating the Student's Work	
			Want to Do More?	

One-Week Lesson Plan

When beginning with Book A, this plan is ideal for most second graders.

Using this plan, you will:

- Do one lesson every week, working four or five days per week.
- Complete all of WriteShop Primary in one year.
  - ~ Book A in 10 weeks
  - ~ Book B in 10 weeks
  - ~ Book C in 10 weeks

The One-Week Lesson Plan sets a faster pace for your second grader. This schedule allows this child to experience all of WriteShop Primary—Books A, B, and C—before starting third grade. You will devote one four-day week to each lesson. (If you would rather have your second grader finish Book C by the end of third grade, use the Two-Week Lesson Plan on p. 5.)

By starting an average to accelerated second grader in Book A, every skill is learned or reinforced as you build upon earlier lessons. By doing so, every skill is learned as you build upon earlier lessons. Even though some of the early lessons may seem basic, you can adjust them to match your student's skill level. For example, let her write independently as much as she can rather than having her dictate her work to you as you might do with a pre-writer.

In order to work at a faster pace, you will double up on activities. Instead of doing one Activity Set each day, you will do two. On Monday, for example, you will complete both Activity Set 1 and Activity Set 2 from the lesson plan. *However, you will not do two Guided Writing Practices each day. Even though the other schedules include eight days of Guided Writing Practice, the One-Week Plan only allows for four.*

The One-Week Lesson Plan for one lesson looks like this:

Monday **Activity Sets 1 & 2**	**Tuesday** **Activity Sets 3 & 4**	**Wednesday** **Activity Sets 5 & 6**	**Thursday** **Activity Sets 7 & 8**	**Friday** **Optional Activities**
Guided Writing Practice	Guided Writing Practice	Guided Writing Practice	Guided Writing Practice	Want to Do More?
Pre-writing Activities	Brainstorming	Editing and Revising	Publishing the Project	
	The Writing Project	Activity Set Worksheet	Evaluating Student's Work	

Flexibility Is Key

No matter which plan you choose, flexibility is the name of the game. If you find that the first several lessons seem too easy for your child, don't hesitate to work at a faster pace. Then, if he begins to struggle as lessons become more challenging, simply switch back to a slower schedule. On the other hand, if he is having a hard time from the beginning, put him on a two-week or three-week plan right away.

Teaching Children at Different Levels

If your young ones are too far apart in age or ability to work at the same level, WriteShop Primary makes it possible to teach two or more children using different books. For example, you might have a:

- Kindergartener in Book A and a second grader in Book B.
- First grader in Book B and a second grader in Book C.
- Kindergartener and first grader in Book A and a third grader in Book C.

Use the Three-Week Plan to complete each book in a year by doing one lesson every three weeks. On the first Monday of a new lesson, plan to do daily Guided Writing Practice with each child according to his own book. Then you can work every other day with each child for the remainder of the lesson.

The Three-Week Plan for two students working in different books looks like this:

	Monday Activity Set 1	**Tuesday Activity Set 2**	**Wednesday Activity Set 2**	**Thursday Activity Set 3**	**Friday Activity Set 3**
Child 1	Guided Writing Practice	Guided Writing Practice Pre-writing Activities	Off	Guided Writing Practice Brainstorming	Off
Child 2	Guided Writing Practice	Off	Guided Writing Practice Pre-writing Activities	Off	Guided Writing Practice Brainstorming

	Monday Activity Set 4	**Tuesday Activity Set 4**	**Wednesday Activity Set 5**	**Thursday Activity Set 5**	**Friday Activity Set 6**
Child 1	Guided Writing Practice The Writing Project	Off	Guided Writing Practice Editing and Revising	Off	Guided Writing Practice Activity Set Worksheet
Child 2	Off	Guided Writing Practice The Writing Project	Off	Guided Writing Practice Editing and Revising	Off

	Monday Activity Set 6	**Tuesday Activity Set 7**	**Wednesday Activity Set 7**	**Thursday Activity Set 8**	**Friday Activity Set 8**
Child 1	Off	Guided Writing Practice Publishing the Project	Off	Guided Writing Practice Evaluating Student's Work Want to Do More?	Off
Child 2	Guided Writing Practice Activity Set Worksheet	Off	Guided Writing Practice Publishing the Project	Off	Guided Writing Practice Evaluating Student's Work Want to Do More?

Materials and Supplies

Getting Ready

To foster the creative writing process, provide a place that is quiet and organized. Following are some ideas for establishing such an environment, as well as step-by-step instructions on how to use WriteShop Primary. If you're teaching a class, you'll find these ideas equally adaptable to a classroom setting.

Let's get started!

Locating Materials and Supplies

Most materials and writing supplies for WriteShop Primary can be found at any office supply store. However, some specific (but optional) items that will greatly enhance the learning environment for your child can only be found at a teacher or school supply store. If you don't have one in your area, visit online stores such as:

- Miller Pads & Paper at **www.millerpadsandpaper.com**
- HomeschoolingSupply.com at **www.homeschoolingsupply.com**
- Lakeshore Learning Materials at **www.lakeshorelearning.com**

The beginning of each lesson includes a list of materials needed for that assignment. In the Appendix, you will also find a master list of materials needed for all of Book A to help you plan ahead.

Activity Set Worksheets

In addition to your Teacher's Manual, you will need an Activity Set Worksheet Pack. This dual-purpose resource contains:

- Activity pages that tie together and reinforce the skills taught in each lesson.
- Two lesson-specific Primary Writing Skills Evaluation Charts to help you track your child's progress.

Creating a Writing Center

To encourage creativity and good work habits for your budding author, it's wise to have a comfortable writing center. Whether you work at the kitchen table or set aside a separate writing area in your home or school classroom, make it as inviting and inspiring as possible to spark the imagination and foster a love for the written word.

Equipping Your Writing Center

Gather the following supplies and store them in your portable or permanent writing center. Keep a completely separate set of supplies in the writing center so they're always handy.

Manuscript Alphabet Chart

- Upper and lower case letters
- Post nearby at the child's eye level

Chart Paper or Newsprint Pad

- This type of paper is used for the daily Guided Writing Practice activity.
- Chart paper comes lined or unlined and is spiral-bound for easy turning. Typically, chart paper is 2-hole punched with stiff covers for hanging or setting on an easel.
- Newsprint pads or tablets come in various sizes. Though they are usually unlined, you can also find lined ones. Depending on the size you choose, you may clip a newsprint pad to an easel or lay it flat on a table top.
- You can also use individual sheets of newsprint, either clipped to an easel or laid flat on a table top.

Writing Tools (organized in bins or tubbies)

- Crayons, markers, pencils, pens
- Rubber stamps, stickers
- Assorted paper (grade-level lined, unlined, construction paper, and patterned paper, as well as novelty papers in a variety of themes)
- Correction tape

Manila File Folders for Portable Word Banks

Portable Word Banks are a great resource for budding writers. Beginning in Lesson 5 and throughout the upcoming lessons of WriteShop Primary, make as many theme-related *Portable Word Banks* as you can with your child.. She can use them as a handy reference while she writes. Simply glue a picture on the front of a manila file folder, add a title, and write a themed list of words inside. *Portable Word Banks* are simple to make and easy to use. These wonderful tools help build vocabulary, spelling,

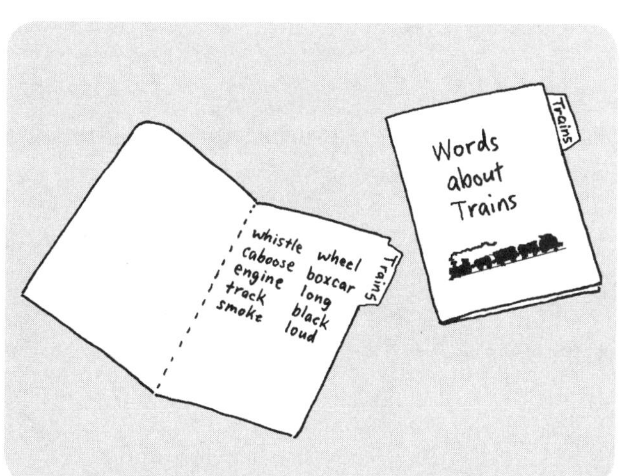

reading, and writing skills for primary students.

For handy storage, label the tab with the title of the word bank and store the folders in a file box. Encourage your child to use these folders for future writing assignments.

Publishing Tools (organized in bins or tubbies)

- Glue, glue sticks, tape
- Scissors, stapler, hole punch, yarn scraps
- Construction paper or scrapbooking paper
- Old magazines, calendars, toy catalogs to cut and paste
- Additional materials as suggested in each lesson

Table or Desk

- Provides a workspace for the child to write each assignment
- Provides a place to complete artwork used in the process of publishing the project

Floor or Table-top Easel (optional)

- Clips to hold chart paper or large sheets of newsprint
- Shelf to hold optional dry-erase board and markers
- Hooks to hold optional pocket chart

Pocket Chart and Sentence Strips (optional)

A pocket chart is a sheet of sturdy fabric with clear plastic see-through pockets. The pockets hold strips of paper on which you've written sentences or words or pictures. Pre-made sentence strips are pieces of sturdy tagboard cut into strips that fit into the pockets. You'll want the simplest 10-pocket chart with long, clear pockets all the way across. You do not need a fancy one with fabric pockets for storage or sideways pockets to slide things along.

For great deals on sentence strips and pocket charts, visit **www.eBay.com.** There are many kinds of pocket charts, so we suggest searching for "standard pocket chart" or "sentence strip pocket chart." Alternatively, you can get these items from a school supply resource.

The pocket chart can easily become the focus of your writing center. Clip it to a large easel, mount it on a bulletin board at your child's height, or hang it from a purchased stand.

The pocket chart also makes a valuable tool for teaching reading, phonics, math, literature, and science. Your child will be eager to use it with you, a big plus for your learning environment.

Idea books yield many more suggestions for incorporating this wonderful tool into your teaching. You can find books online, through school supply stores, or via a Google search for "pocket chart ideas" or "pocket chart activities."

If you choose not to use a pocket chart in your writing center because of space restrictions or other reasons, that's fine! You can still do the occasional suggested pocket chart activities in these lessons. Simply write the words and phrases on lined paper and cut them into strips that you and your child can move around on a flat surface.

Storage Suggestions

There are many ways to organize and store your materials, depending on your homeschooling style, how much room you have in your home, etc. Here are some storage options when creating a writing center.

Portable Writing Center

- Large backpack with pockets
- Bucket tool organizer (such as a cleaning supply caddy)
- Large plastic box with hinged or snap-on lid

Semi-permanent or Permanent Writing Center

- Over-the-door pocket shoe organizer
- Bookshelf
- Stacking letter trays for paper
- Cubbies, tubs, bins, or baskets

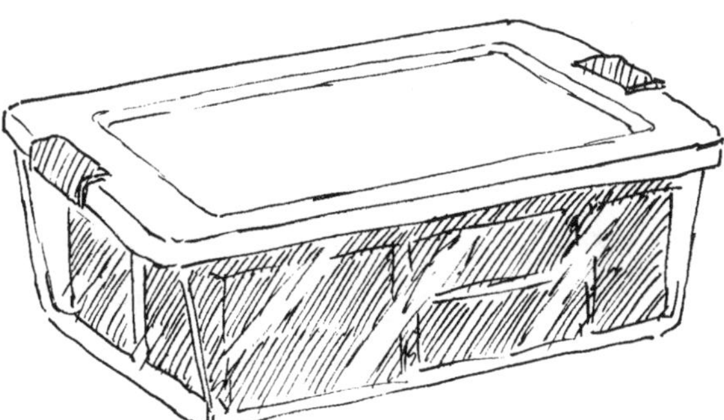

Teaching the Lessons

According to your chosen schedule, you will complete each WriteShop Primary lesson in one, two, or three weeks. Look for these elements in each and every lesson.

Lesson Focus

Every WriteShop Primary Lesson teaches a new writing skill to your child. You will find the Lesson Focus at the beginning of each lesson. Lesson Focus examples include:

- *Lesson 4:* Selecting a Title
- *Lesson 8:* Using a Story Web to Organize Ideas
- *Lesson 10:* Writing about Events in the Order They Happen

Lesson Theme

Lessons in Book A are based around a theme. This makes assignments more interesting and helps tie all the activities together. The elements of each lesson, including the picture book choice, topic of the Writing Project, and Activity Set Worksheets will support the theme.

The beginning of each lesson lists the theme. Examples include:

- *Lesson 1*: Animals
- *Lesson 5:* Trains
- *Lesson 7:* Rhymes

Choosing an Alternate Theme

WriteShop Primary's lesson themes have been carefully chosen to meet standards for grades K-3. However, many homeschooling families like to teach with unit studies, where they try to center all subjects on their current area of interest. If a WriteShop Primary theme does not fit well with your unit study, it is sometimes possible to substitute a similar topic. For example, Lesson 8's theme is Insects and Bugs. But what if you are learning about birds at that time?

Instead of…	*You can…*
Making an insect house	Make a birdhouse
Reading a book about ladybugs	Read a book about parrots
Going on an insect walk	Take a bird walk

Although choosing an alternate theme will not work every time, this example shows one way you can tweak WriteShop Primary to suit your family's needs.

Lesson Objectives

The beginning of each lesson includes a set of objectives that your child will strive for. For example, your child might:

- Write information about herself.

- Use order words to describe a sequence of events.
- Identify punctuation marks.

Materials

The beginning of each lesson includes a list of materials needed for that assignment. If your Writing Center is well equipped (see pp. 9-11), you should already have most items on hand. It's a good idea to gather any extra supplies in advance so you're not scrambling at the last minute. In the Appendix, you will also find a master list of materials needed for the entire scope of the program to help you plan ahead.

Your materials list will also tell you what kind of picture book(s) you need for that lesson. Again, plan ahead in case you need to search your home bookshelf, make a trip to the library, or order books online.

Advance Prep

From time to time, certain activities will be preceded by a text box containing Advance Prep instructions. These boxes let you know that you must make a few simple preparations before your child can do the activity. Examples of Advance Prep include:

- Cutting out paper shapes.
- Gathering a few simple supplies.
- Making pointers.

If you have gathered your materials and supplies ahead of time, you won't be caught off guard when an Advance Prep text box appears. Giving yourself a few minutes to properly prepare will ensure that your child receives the most benefit from her lesson.

One idea: Use an accordion file or individual file folders (labeled Lesson 1, Lesson 2, etc.) to prepare and store Advance Prep materials as time permits.

Activity Sets

Activity Sets Overview

WriteShop Primary Lessons provide a comfortable and predictable routine for you and your child. Each lesson is split into eight Activity Sets consisting of Guided Writing Practice and (with the exception of Activity Set 1) one or more exercises. No matter which lesson you are working on, Activity Sets will always contain the same elements listed below. The track or schedule you choose (pp. 3-7) will tell you how many Activity Sets to do each week.

Activity Set 1

- Guided Writing Practice

Activity Set 2

- Guided Writing Practice
- Pre-writing Activities
  - ~ Picture Book to Read Aloud
  - ~ Related Warm-up Games or Exercises

Activity Set 3

- Guided Writing Practice
- Brainstorming

Activity Set 4

- Guided Writing Practice
- The Writing Project
  - ~ Writing the First Draft
  - ~ Smaller Steps (suggestions for younger writers)
  - ~ Flying Higher (suggestions for more fluent or advanced writers)

Activity Set 5

- Guided Writing Practice
- Editing and Revising the First Draft

Activity Set 6

- Guided Writing Practice
- Activity Set Worksheet

Activity Set 7

- Guided Writing Practice
- Publishing the Project (final draft)

Activity Set 8

- Guided Writing Practice
- Evaluating the Student's Work
- Want to Do More? (optional activities)
  - ~ Writing Across the Curriculum
  - ~ Computer Capers

Activity Sets Numbering System

Activity Sets are numbered within each lesson to help you find them quickly. If you are working in Lesson 1, for example, Activity Sets 1, 2, and 3 will be identified as Activity Sets 1:1, 1:2, and 1:3.

You will find this numbering system especially useful when a lesson refers you to an earlier exercise or project. For instance, during the Smaller Steps exercise in Lesson 7, you will read: *If she hasn't already made one, follow the instructions in Activity Set 5:8 to make a paper wallet or purse and gold coins.* This quickly and simply tells you to return to Lesson 5, Activity Set 8 in order to find the original instructions for this project.

Guided Writing Practice (Daily)

Because children learn best by example, WriteShop Primary shows you how to model correct writing techniques to your child. You will do this during Guided Writing Practice.

Each Activity Set includes Guided Writing Practice, the teaching time and heart of WriteShop Primary. Its purpose is to provide your child with a daily, predictable, shared writing experience. During Guided Writing Practice, you and your child will write several short sentences about simple, familiar topics such as *animals, friends, the weather*, or *upcoming events*. We strongly encourage you to attempt every Guided Writing Practice, but if this is not possible, aim to do at least two each week.

At first (Book A), Guided Writing Practice will use fairly predictable sentence starters. Don't let this simplicity fool you into thinking this activity is beneath your child. Guided Writing Practice is a common primary-level teaching tool that simply lays a foundation for writing. In later lessons, as your child's writing skills increase, you will use the Guided Writing Practice time to gradually introduce new concepts such as choosing titles or identifying a story setting.

Keep it short, about 5-10 minutes. This is not the time for writing complicated sentences. It's just for building a simple foundation by modeling daily writing techniques.

Guided Writing Practice

1. Signals the beginning of "writing time" and sets a positive tone for your school day.
2. Gives the child a sense of security through routine.
3. Teaches important writing skills.
    - Left-to-right progression
    - Letter formation
    - Correct spacing
    - Punctuation
    - Word patterns
    - Reading and writing common sight words
4. Plays a role in teaching writing by giving the child daily practice. For beginning readers, the predictable patterns and easy sight words build confidence. For more confident readers, Guided Writing time gives daily practice in reading and writing harder words and sentences.

As you model writing for your child during Guided Writing Practice, use these teaching techniques.

- Start with a blank piece of paper and write with a wide-tipped marker while sitting next to your child or standing at the easel.
- Model writing from left to right and top to bottom.
- As much as possible, include the child in the process of brainstorming and deciding what to write. Ask questions to stimulate ideas. Each Guided Writing Practice will provide you with examples.
- Start these lessons by writing just two or three simple sentences, following the lesson's instructions. Though your sentences may vary, when possible, make sure they relate to the theme of the lesson. In later lessons, you will add more sentences.
- During Guided Writing Practice, you will write most of the text. Do encourage your child to write some of the letters or words she already knows. For instance, if she can write an upper-case "T" or fill in a blank with her name, a specific word, or a high-frequency word such as *and* or *to*, invite her to use the marker and write that letter or word in the sentence.
- For words your child can't write or spell, phonetically sound out the letters as you write the words.
- Guided Writing Practice should not take more than 5-10 minutes. If your child is an older or stronger

writer and wants to write most of the words during Guided Writing Practice, by all means let her—as long as you set a time limit. And if time begins to run short, share the rest of the writing with her. Remember that she will have plenty of other opportunities to write during each lesson and shouldn't use up all her writing energy on this one activity.

- After your Guided Writing Practice is written on paper, read it two times. First, read the passage aloud to your child in its entirety. Next, read the sentences together, pointing to each word and encouraging her to read any words that she knows.
- Discuss the main idea and add a title.

Sometimes children get stuck and can't think of what they want to say. Other times they ramble and use run-on sentences. If your child has trouble, you will need to guide her. Pause to prompt her with questions and ask for clarification. Your Guided Writing prompting will vary. It will be more predictable and simpler in early lessons, becoming more detailed and specific later on. To give you ideas, each lesson will have at least one Guided Writing sample or dialogue.

Above all, have fun with Guided Writing Practice—your positive attitude makes all the difference. View this as a pleasurable teaching time. Most children find it fun, challenging and engaging. They love to talk about their friends, family, and daily happenings—frequent Guided Writing topics—and they love to spend time with you.

Most importantly, this gives them the freedom to put together ideas and create word patterns without the limitations and fear of having to write them down. Understand how important it is to dialogue with your child. Speak encouragingly to her and show her that you value what she has to say.

After your writing lesson is over for the day, think about keeping each day's page. At the end of WriteShop Primary Book A, bind the pages together to make a big book. Since most Guided Writing topics focus on the child's world—her home, family, and day-to-day experiences—this book will become a wonderful diary for her to enjoy.

Pre-writing Activities (Activity Set 2)

Every lesson helps you prepare your child to write by reading a picture book together. Many lessons also offer related warm-up games and exercises.

Expose your child to quality writing. On the second day of each new lesson, read a picture book aloud to him. Keep it short, however. Save longer books for later in the day when you have time to sit down in a relaxing atmosphere and read aloud for a full fifteen or thirty minutes.

For now, you are simply helping him prepare to write. Choose a short, engaging, age-appropriate picture book with lots of bright colors and vivid illustrations.

Be sure you read during this time, not your child. There will be plenty of other times for him to practice reading skills.

To find a variety of picture books, visit the children's section of your library. If you want to build a library at home, you can find inexpensive used picture books at yard sales, library sales, and online stores (like **www.Amazon.com** or **www.half.com**). For book suggestions, see pages 181-83 in the Appendix or visit **www.writeshop.com/picturebooks.htm**

Brainstorming (Activity Set 3)

Brainstorming is a key ingredient of the creative writing process. With primary students, this is usually a shared experience, guided by the teacher. Before beginning each lesson's writing project, brainstorm with your child for ideas related to that day's topic.

You and your child will use brainstorming to:

- Generate lists of topic ideas for writing.
- Determine things to write about his chosen topic.

Why brainstorm?

- Helps your child focus his attention on the topic.
- Generates a number of different ideas.
- Encourages your child to share his ideas and opinions without fear of criticism.
- Shows your child that he will have more to say during writing time if he has already given his topic some thought.

The most basic form of brainstorming is to make a list of ideas. Write these ideas on a tablet while sitting with your child or on chart paper at an easel. Keep this list handy throughout the rest of the lesson to help spark ideas during the writing stage and extended activities. In later lessons, your child will learn to use other brainstorming methods, such as story webs and a *Story Idea Card File*.

What is the simple secret of brainstorming? Don't pressure your child to be "right." Simply let him focus on a topic and share whatever pops into his mind. During this time, allow a free flow of ideas. Your child will not use every idea he comes up with, but that's okay.

During brainstorming, encourage your student to think creatively and use his imagination. Don't criticize ideas that seem off-topic. What a child pictures in his mind may be hard to communicate effectively at this point. Gently guide him in a positive way until he is able to make suggestions that support the main idea.

The Writing Project (Activity Set 4)

The Writing Project is the central focus of each lesson. Everything you have done so far, from guided writing to brainstorming, has paved the way for the Writing Project. This is where the child will apply his newly learned skills by writing sentences and stories.

At the primary level, and especially in the first few lessons of WriteShop Primary, the creative writing projects focus mainly on pre-writing skills. First, most children at this level do not have the ability to write many words. Second, they are just beginning to learn new skills of punctuation, capitalization, and grammar. The tools your child gains during these lessons are the building blocks that prepare him for future creative writing exercises. As his knowledge and abilities increase, he will begin to write (and eventually publish) his very own stories.

According to his ability, your student will either dictate his story to you or write it independently.

Pre-writers

- A pre-writer can dictate his thoughts to you while you write his words and sentences on a piece of paper. This is an important step in preparing to write! He sees that the words he speaks can be written down and shared with others to read.
- As his writing skills mature, invite your child to participate more and more in the writing process.

Beginning Writers

- If your student is already writing, encourage independence as much as possible.
- Allow him to dictate whatever he cannot write by himself.

Advanced Writers

- A more fluent writer can expand the basic Writing Project concept by writing at his level of ability.
- However, don't discount the value of taking dictation from such a child. Often, a child's oral vocabulary is more advanced than his ability to write. You may find that his stories are more colorful and descriptive when he dictates them to you.
- If you do take dictation from a more advanced child, he can recopy "his words" onto a separate sheet of paper later.

Smaller Steps or Flying Higher

Younger or struggling children may need extra help with their Writing Project. See the Smaller Steps box in each lesson for suggestions on how to adapt the lesson. Likewise, for advanced students, the Flying Higher box will suggest activities to make the Writing Project more challenging.

Here are some examples.

- *Smaller Steps (Lesson 1):* A younger learner may benefit from using this time to practice memorizing his address and phone number.
- *Smaller Steps (Lesson 3):* As a younger child dictates, write down her story in large, bold letters. Help her track the letters as you write. Don't use tiny print, all-capital letters, or cursive handwriting.
- *Flying Higher (Lesson 2):* An advanced or accelerated student may want to add more pages, perhaps incorporating the ideas she will choose for her Activity Set Worksheet (favorite place, toy, or book). She might also add more pages about why she's special.
- *Flying Higher (Lesson 4):* Use a children's dictionary with an advanced or accelerated student to look up the meaning of unfamiliar words. Introduce a thesaurus to him and find new words to describe friends.

Editing and Revising (Activity Set 5)

Editing does not need to be a negative or intimidating experience. When children learn at a young age the value of gentle correction and self-improvement, they will come to see editing as a natural part of the writing process.

During this activity, your child will learn to look for ways to improve her Writing Project. The amount of editing will increase as lessons progress and the child matures. In the beginning, the focus is on content.

Mechanics is secondary. For example, at this stage of writing, you may begin to notice your child spelling "by ear" or inventing her own spellings. Don't worry too much about spelling mistakes or poorly formed letters; it doesn't mean she'll learn the words incorrectly or develop bad handwriting habits. These skills will come later.

Help your child evaluate her own work. If she needs to make changes on her project, this is the time to do so. Do not cross out or erase; simply print the new word(s) directly above the old one(s). Later, as lessons progress, the child will have the opportunity to rewrite some of her projects on fresh paper, should she so choose.

Activity Set Worksheets (Activity Set 6)

Activity Pages

The Activity Set Worksheet Pack offers consumable activity pages that tie together and reinforce the skills taught in each lesson. These worksheets are not meant to stand alone. Therefore, don't plan to use them as a busy-day replacement for other lesson activities. Instead, view them as materials that support what you have already taught.

Here are just a few of the ways your student will use the worksheets.

- Learn new words and build vocabulary.
- Make a story web and organize brainstorming ideas.
- Apply newly learned concepts to the writing lesson.
- Publish a writing project.

In the beginning, these worksheets may seem too easy for a more advanced child. That's okay—you'll find that within just a few lessons, the activities become more challenging. Meanwhile, simply let him have fun! For most children, these pages help them learn some very basic truths about writing—that it doesn't have to be scary or intimidating, and it doesn't have to be hard.

The reverse side of many of the Activity Set Worksheets has space for your child to independently practice handwriting, spelling, or other basic writing skills. Unlike the Writing Project, which will undergo minor editing and revising, the Activity Set Worksheets are for practice only. To help your young writer feel safe trying out new skills, you will not be correcting these pages.

Evaluation Pages

In the Activity Set Worksheet Pack you'll find two Primary Writing Skills Evaluation Charts. To learn how to use these charts, see "Evaluating Your Child's Work," p. 20.

Publishing the Project (Activity Set 7)

One of the most encouraging and rewarding experiences for a young author is to see her work published. WriteShop Primary gives your student the opportunity to publish her Writing Project as a book or other art form that she can share with others. Most children love this creative activity.

Here are some fun ways your child will publish her Writing Projects.

- Make a kite.

- Create a paper plate "face" book.
- Make an accordion-folded train book.

While children usually love to combine writing and art to create their final drafts, your child may not like craft projects as much. Or perhaps you're not a crafty person and would rather bypass the hands-on activities because they're not your style. Know that it's okay to let her skip this activity once in a while, but do encourage her to publish most of the projects.

Also, to reinforce the concept of editing and revising, make sure that whenever you do let her skip an art-related publishing project, she must still produce a final draft by neatly rewriting her Writing Project story on lined paper.

Evaluating Your Child's Work (Activity Set 8)

In the Activity Set Worksheet Pack, you will find Primary Writing Skills Evaluation Charts. Each chart tracks the progress of five lessons. Remove the corresponding chart from the pack at the beginning of Lessons 1 and 6. Keep the progress charts in your notebook or file.

The Primary Writing Skills Evaluation Chart is not meant as a grading tool. Rather, it's a way to record your child's growth and gain a better grasp of his strengths and weaknesses. In upcoming lessons, you can then focus on those skills that need improvement.

Since WriteShop Primary is an incremental writing program, you will evaluate new skills as your child is introduced to them in upcoming lessons. This will help you determine whether or not your child is acquiring each building block she needs on her creative writing journey.

The philosophy of WriteShop Primary is that students in kindergarten through third grade don't need letter grades for creative writing. Your school or support group may have specific guidelines regarding grading requirements. If this is the case, you will need to determine what type of records they expect you to keep.

Want to Do More? (Activity Set 8)

At the end of every WriteShop Primary lesson, you will find optional activities called Want to Do More? Motivated or accelerated children will definitely enjoy these extra assignments. Reluctant learners may also benefit from participating now and then, so from time to time, consider including a Want to Do More? activity in your writing schedule.

Writing Across the Curriculum
Creative writing flows well from one subject to another. Writing can be integrated with science, social studies, history, and even math. At the end of each lesson, children will have the option to write across the curriculum by exploring creative writing within a specific subject matter. These optional Want to Do More? activities and projects also offer an excellent challenge for more advanced students.

Computer Capers
An occasional Want to Do More? computer activity will be offered for children who want to practice creative writing skills while learning to work on a computer.

Lesson 1: Welcome to WriteShop Primary

Lesson Focus: Getting Started
Theme: Animals

Objectives

Your child will:

- Become familiar with the general structure of the lessons for WriteShop Primary.
- Be introduced to the concept of brainstorming for ideas on a given topic.
- Observe the relationship between verbal and written expressions.

Materials

Guided Writing Practice

- Tablet or chart paper and markers

Pre-writing Activities

- Picture book about one specific animal

Brainstorming

- Tablet or chart paper and markers

The Writing Project

- 12- x 18-inch construction paper
- Crayons or markers

Activity Set Worksheet

- Crayons or markers

Publishing the Project

- Paper streamers (crêpe-paper party streamers or strips of tissue paper)
- Yarn
- Stapler, scissors, clear tape, hole punch

Want to Do More?

- Writing Across the Curriculum
  - ~ 12- x 18-inch construction paper
  - ~ Crayons or markers

Planning Your Schedule

If you haven't already done so, refer to the charts on pp. 3-7 and select a plan to follow.

Instructions for Lesson 1 begin on page 23. Every lesson has eight Activity Sets. The plan you choose tells you how many Activity Sets to do each week.

Three-Week Lesson Plan

If you follow the Three-Week Plan, you will spend three weeks on each lesson, working three days each week. Your schedule will typically look like this:

- *Week 1*
  - ~ Monday: Activity Set 1
  - ~ Wednesday: Activity Set 2
  - ~ Friday: Activity Set 3
- *Week 2*
  - ~ Monday: Activity Set 4
  - ~ Wednesday: Activity Set 5
  - ~ Friday: Activity Set 6
- *Week 3*
  - ~ Monday: Activity Set 7
  - ~ Wednesday: Activity Set 8
  - ~ Friday: Off

Two-Week Lesson Plan

If you follow the Two-Week Plan, you will spend two weeks on each lesson, working four days each week. Your schedule will typically look like this:

- *Week 1*
  - ~ Monday: Activity Set 1
  - ~ Tuesday: Activity Set 2
  - ~ Wednesday: Activity Set 3
  - ~ Thursday: Activity Set 4
- *Week 2*
  - ~ Monday: Activity Set 5
  - ~ Tuesday: Activity Set 6
  - ~ Wednesday: Activity Set 7
  - ~ Thursday: Activity Set 8

One-Week Plan

If you follow the One-Week Plan, you will spend one week on each lesson, working four days each week. If you want, you can use Friday for the optional Want to Do More? activities. Your schedule will typically look like this:

- *Monday:* Activity Sets 1 and 2
- *Tuesday:* Activity Sets 3 and 4
- *Wednesday:* Activity Sets 5 and 6
- *Thursday:* Activity Sets 7 and 8
- *Friday:* Want to Do More? (optional activities)

ACTIVITY SET 1:1

Guided Writing Practice

At a Glance: Activity Set 1:1

- Guided Writing Practice

Review the Guided Writing Practice guidelines on pp. 13-15 of the Introduction. You will do a Guided Writing Practice every day according to your chosen lesson plan, so you'll want to understand the method as well as the purpose for this important exercise. Guided Writing Practice is not meant to be an in-depth activity. Spend no more than 5-10 minutes, resisting the temptation to make it complicated or time-consuming. We strongly encourage you to attempt every Guided Writing Practice, but if this is not possible, aim to do at least two each week.

Sit down with your child for today's Guided Writing Practice. You may sit side-by-side and write on a tablet or you may use an easel with chart paper. The theme of this lesson is animals. On the first day of the lesson, during Guided Writing Practice, write about pets your family owns. If you don't have a pet, write about pets your child's friends or grandparents have.

First write a short title at the top. Tell your child, "Let's think about the pets that live at our house." (or at Grandma's house or Maya's house). Talk about pets and write down several simple sentences. Model writing for your child as explained in the Introduction, sharing the marker so he writes as many of the letters or words as he knows how.

If your child gives one- or two-word answers, prompt him to give a complete thought. You might want to follow this example for today's Guided Writing Practice.

You: *Let's write a title for today's writing time. We'll call it "Our Pets."*

You: *How many pets do we have?*

Child: Two.

You: *That's right! Now, tell me your answer as a complete thought. We have two pets. Say that. "We have two pets."*

Child: We have two pets.

You: *Super! That's called a complete sentence. Let's write that down on our paper. We have two pets.*

You: *What's one kind of pet we have?*

Child: A goldfish.

You: *That's right. Now let's make a complete thought. We have a goldfish. Say that. "We have a goldfish."*

Child: We have a goldfish.

You: *Excellent! Let's write it down. We have a goldfish.*

You: *How do we feel about pets?*

Child: We like our pets.

You: We sure do! Let's write that sentence. We like our pets.

Here's an example of a completed Guided Writing Practice.

Our Pets
We have two pets.
We have a goldfish.
We like our pets.

After your Guided Writing Practice is written on paper, read it two times. First, read the passage aloud to your child in its entirety. Next, read the sentences together, pointing to each word and encouraging your child to read any words that she knows.

Remember that this example is only a guide. Your goal is to explain the topic you will be writing about each day and encourage your child to suggest simple sentences for you to write together on the chart paper.

ACTIVITY SET 1:2

wednesday / monday

Guided Writing Practice

> **At a Glance: Activity Set 1:2**
> - Guided Writing Practice
> - Pre-writing Activities: Picture Book about an Animal

Sit down with your child for today's Guided Writing Practice. You may sit side-by-side and write on a tablet or you may use an easel with chart paper. Spend 5-10 minutes on this activity.

Remember that you'll probably need to prompt your child in order to get complete sentences from her. Tell your child, "Let's think of animals that people like to have as pets." You might want to follow this example for today's Guided Writing Practice.

You: *Let's write a title for today's writing time. We'll call it "New Pets."*

You: *What kind of pet do you want?*

Child: I want a horse.

You: *What other kind of pet might you like?*

Child: I might like a frog.

You: *What other kind of pet would be nice?*

Child: A puppy would be nice.

Here's an example of a completed Guided Writing Practice.

<u>New Pets</u>
I want a horse.
I might like a frog.
A puppy would be nice.

After your Guided Writing Practice is written on paper, read it two times. First, read the passage aloud to your child in its entirety. Next, read the sentences together, pointing to each word and encouraging your child to read any words that she knows.

Pre-writing Activities

Picture Book about an Animal

Read a picture book aloud to your child about an animal. When finished, discuss what makes that particular animal special and unique from all the other kinds.

ACTIVITY SET 1:3

Friday / Tuesday

Guided Writing Practice

Sit down with your child for today's Guided Writing Practice. You may sit side-by-side and write on a tablet or you may use an easel with chart paper. Spend 5-10 minutes on this activity.

At a Glance: Activity Set 1:3

- Guided Writing Practice
- Brainstorming

Tell your child, "Let's think of animals that would make very strange pets!" Continue prompting your child to give a complete thought. You could use the following example for today's Guided Writing Practice, prompting her with words like *big, tall, hairy, silly, wet, noisy,* or *slippery.* Here's how:

You:	*Let's write a title for today's writing time. We'll call it "Strange Pets."*
You:	*What strange animal would make a* big *pet?*
Child:	A hippo would make a big pet.
You:	*What strange animal would make a* funny *pet?*
Child:	A monkey would make a funny pet.
You:	*What strange animal would make a* scary *pet?*
Child:	A dinosaur would make a scary pet.

Here's an example of a completed Guided Writing Practice.

Strange Pets
A hippo would make a big pet.
A monkey would make a funny pet.
A dinosaur would make a scary pet.

After your Guided Writing Practice is written on paper, read it aloud two times as you have done on previous days.

Brainstorming - Making a List

Ask your child to tell you his favorite kinds of animals. On a tablet or on chart paper, write down a list of these animals.

ACTIVITY SET 1:4

Guided Writing Practice

Sit down with your child for today's Guided Writing Practice. You may sit side-by-side and write on a tablet or you may use an easel with chart paper. Spend 5-10 minutes on this activity. Continuing with the lesson theme, suggest an animal-related topic from this list:

At a Glance: Activity Set 1:4

- Guided Writing Practice
- The Writing Project
- Smaller Steps or Flying Higher

Lesson 1 Topic Ideas for Guided Writing Practice

Desert Animals
Silly Animals
Make-Believe Animals
My Favorite Animals
Animals at the Zoo
My Stuffed Animals
Animals at the Circus
Ocean Creatures
Different Kinds of Cats
Who Lives at the Pet Store?
Animals That Swim (Fly, Climb)
Farm Animals
Animal Babies

Use prompts similar to the ones from previous days. Here is one suggestion.

You: *Let's write a title for today's writing time. We'll call it "Farm Animals."*
You: *What is a* fluffy *farm animal?*
Child: A lamb is a fluffy farm animal.
You: *What is a* loud *farm animal?*
Child: A rooster is a loud farm animal.
You: *What is a* messy *farm animal?*
Child: A pig is a messy farm animal.

Here's an example of a completed Guided Writing Practice:

Farm Animals
A lamb is a fluffy farm animal.
A rooster is a loud farm animal.
A pig is a messy farm animal.

After your Guided Writing Practice is written on paper, read it aloud two times as you have done on previous days.

The Writing Project - My Favorite Animal

Directions

1. Help your child refer to the list of brainstorming ideas to choose what she will draw.
2. Ask her to draw a picture of one of her favorite animals on a 12- x 18-inch piece of construction paper.
3. After her picture is finished, prompt her with positive statements or questions such as, "Tell me about your picture," or "Can you tell me more?" Discreetly avoid asking, "What is it?"
4. Have her dictate a sentence for you to write across the bottom of the page, such as: My favorite animal is a/an _________.

Smaller Steps - Using a Picture as a Prompt

For a younger student, look at a picture of the animal before drawing it.

Flying Higher - Creating an Animal Story

For an advanced or accelerated student, have her create a story about the animal and dictate it to you. Write her story on a separate piece of paper. If your child is already an independent writer, she can write the words instead of dictating them to you.

ACTIVITY SET 1:5

Guided Writing Practice

Sit down with your child for today's Guided Writing Practice. You may sit side-by-side and write on a tablet or you may use an easel with chart paper. Spend 5-10 minutes on this activity.

> **At a Glance: Activity Set 1:5**
> - Guided Writing Practice
> - Editing and Revising

Suggest a new animal-related topic from the list on page 27. Use prompts similar to the ones from previous days. Here is one suggestion.

You: *Let's write a title for today's writing time. We'll call it "Ocean Creatures."*

You: *What big creature lives in the ocean?*

Child: A whale lives in the ocean.

You: *What ocean creature lives in a shell?*

Child: A crab lives in a shell.

You: *What is a colorful ocean creature?*

Child: A clownfish is a colorful ocean creature.

Here's an example of a completed Guided Writing Practice.

Ocean Creatures
A whale lives in the ocean.
A crab lives in a shell.
A clownfish is a colorful ocean creature.

Read the completed Guided Writing Practice aloud two times as you have done on previous days.

Editing and Revising

Sit down with your child and her Writing Project.

1. Ask your child to tell you what her drawing is all about.
2. Together, read the sentence written across the bottom of the page. Ask her if her sentence or story tells about the picture she drew. If not, ask her if there are any changes that could be made to express what she wants to say in a better way.
3. If changes need to be made on the project, this is the time to do so.

ACTIVITY SET 1:6

Guided Writing Practice

Sit down with your child for today's Guided Writing Practice. You may sit side-by-side and write on a tablet or you may use an easel with chart paper. Spend 5-10 minutes on this activity.

Suggest a new animal-related topic from the list on page 27. Use similar prompts to the ones from previous days. Here is one suggestion.

> **At a Glance: Activity Set 1:6**
>
> - Guided Writing Practice
> - Activity Set Worksheet: "Animal Fun"

You:	*Let's write a title for today's writing time. We'll call it "My Stuffed Animals."*
You:	*How many stuffed animals do you have?*
Child:	I have nine stuffed animals.
You:	*Which is your softest stuffed animal?*
Child:	My cat is my softest stuffed animal.
You:	*Which stuffed animal do you like to sleep with?*
Child:	I like to sleep with Tusky.

Here's an example of a completed Guided Writing Practice.

My Stuffed Animals
I have nine stuffed animals.
My cat is my softest stuffed animal.
I like to sleep with Tusky.

After your Guided Writing Practice is written on paper, read it aloud two times as you have done on previous days.

Activity Set Worksheet - "Animal Fun"

Use Lesson 1: "Animal Fun" Activity Set Worksheet.

1. Help your child sound out and trace the first letter of each animal's name.
2. Have him choose an animal from the Word Bank, write that animal's name in the blank space, and draw a picture of it.
3. On the back of the worksheet, encourage him to practice writing the beginning letter or name of some of the other animals from the Word Bank.

ACTIVITY SET 1:7

Guided Writing Practice

Sit down with your child for today's Guided Writing Practice. You may sit side-by-side and write on a tablet or you may use an easel with chart paper. Spend 5-10 minutes on this activity.

At a Glance: Activity Set 1:7

- Guided Writing Practice
- Publishing the Project

Suggest a new animal-related topic from the list on page 27. Use similar prompts to the ones from previous days. Here is one suggestion.

You:	*Let's write a title for today's writing time. We'll call it "Animals at the Circus."*
You:	*Do you remember our library book about the circus?*
Child:	Yes.
You:	*Help me remember one kind of circus animal that can dance.*
Child:	A little dog can dance.
You:	*What kind of circus animal can people ride on?*
Child:	People can ride on an elephant.
You:	*What kind of circus animal might be a dangerous animal?*
Child:	A lion might be a dangerous animal.

Here's an example of a completed Guided Writing Practice.

> Animals at the Circus
> A little dog can dance.
> People can ride on an elephant.
> A lion might be a dangerous animal.

After your Guided Writing Practice is written on paper, read it aloud two times as you have done on previous days.

Publishing the Project - Making a Story Kite

To publish the Writing Project from Activity Set 1:4, make it into a kite. Here's how:

1. Staple or tape the opposite ends of the picture together to form a cylinder.
2. Tape four 12-inch paper streamers to the bottom of the cylinder. (If cutting your own, make them about three inches wide.)

3. Use a hole-punch to punch two holes opposite each other at the top of the cylinder. Reinforce holes with tape or paper hole reinforcements.
4. Tie on a yarn handle.
5. Provide time now or later in the day for your child to "fly" his kite to you or to someone else he wants to share it with.
6. Encourage him to read the sentence aloud and explain the picture.

ACTIVITY SET 1:8

Guided Writing Practice

Sit down with your child for today's Guided Writing Practice. You may sit side-by-side and write on a tablet or you may use an easel with chart paper. Spend 5-10 minutes on this activity.

At a Glance: Activity Set 1:8

- Guided Writing Practice
- Evaluating the Student's Work
- Want to Do More? (optional) Writing Across the Curriculum: Spotlight on Math

Suggest a new animal-related topic from the list on page 27. Use similar prompts to the ones from previous days. Here is one suggestion.

You: *Let's write a title for today's writing time. We'll call it "Animal Babies."*

You: *What is a baby dog called?*

Child: A baby dog is called a puppy.

You: *What is a baby kangaroo called?*

Child: A baby kangaroo is called a joey.

You: *What is your favorite animal baby?*

Child: My favorite animal baby is a bunny.

You: *Why do you like baby animals?*

Child: I like baby animals because they're soft and small.

Here's an example of a completed Guided Writing Practice:

Animal Babies
A baby dog is called a puppy.
A baby kangaroo is called a joey.
My favorite animal baby is a bunny.
I like baby animals because they're soft and small.

After your Guided Writing Practice is written on paper, read it aloud two times as you have done on previous days.

Evaluating the Student's Work

Use the Primary Writing Skills Evaluation Chart for Lessons 1-5 to evaluate your child's work. Remove it from the Activity Set Worksheet Pack and keep it in a notebook or file.

As you fill in the chart, add today's date beneath Lesson 1. Fill in each box according to your child's progress as of today. For example:

- **Writes from left to right.** Ask yourself, "As of today, does Taylor write from left to right MOST of the time, SOME of the time, or NEVER?"
- **Writes sentences.** Ask yourself, "As of today, does Taylor write sentences MOST of the time, SOME of the time, or NEVER?"

Want to Do More?

Writing Across the Curriculum: Spotlight on Math

Directions

1. Give your child a piece of 12- x 18-inch construction paper. Draw two lines on the paper to separate it into four equal quadrants. In the first space write *1* ______. In the second space write *2* ______. In the third space write *3* ______. In the fourth space write *4* ______.
2. Referring to the brainstorming list from Activity Set 1:3 or the Animal Word Bank from the Activity Set Worksheet, have her draw the correct number of matching animals in each space, using a different kind of animal for each number. For example, next to the 1, she might draw one cat. Perhaps she'll draw two dogs next to the 2, followed by three pigs and ending with four bugs. Help your child write the animals' names in the blanks.
3. When finished, ask her to explain to you what makes each group of animals special and unique from the others.

Lesson 2: All About Me

Lesson Focus: Personal Writing
Theme: I Am Special

Objectives

Your child will:

- Write information about himself.
- Learn that each person is unique and that these unique qualities can be expressed through the written word.
- Be introduced to the concept that a sentence conveys a complete thought.
- Discover that his opinions matter and can be shared with others through writing.

Materials

Guided Writing Practice

- Tablet or chart paper and markers

Pre-writing Activities

- Nonfiction picture book or easy reader about a famous person
- Writing paper or pocket chart with sentence strips
- Markers, scissors, glue
- Old magazines

Brainstorming

- Tablet or chart paper and markers
- Digital camera (optional)

The Writing Project

- Five 12- x 18-inch sheets of construction paper in light colors such as white, yellow, or powder blue
- Markers or crayons
- Scissors

Publishing the Project

- 10-inch paper plate
- Scissors, glue, tape, stapler, markers, crayons
- Bits of yarn or fabric

Want to Do More?

- Writing Across the Curriculum
  - ~ Same supplies as the Writing Project
  - ~ Nonfiction magazine article or book about animals
- Computer Capers
  - ~ Children's encyclopedia software or Internet access

ACTIVITY SET 2:1

Guided Writing Practice

At a Glance: Activity Set 2:1

- Guided Writing Practice

Sit side-by-side with your child and write on a tablet, or use an easel with chart paper. Spend 5-10 minutes each session.

Using a marker, write a short title at the top relating to something that is happening today. Discuss these events with your child and write several simple sentences. Model writing for your student as explained in the Introduction, sharing the marker so he writes any letters or words that he knows. Remember that the examples are here to guide and inspire you. Your goal is to explain the topic you will be writing about each day, and to use prompts and questions to draw your child's own responses.

You will probably need to prompt your child in order to get complete sentences from him. Here is one suggestion.

You:	*Let's write a title for today's writing time. We'll call it "A Visit."*
You:	*Let's look at the calendar. What day is today?*
Child:	Today is Monday.
You:	*Tell me one thing that will happen today.*
Child:	Grandma is coming to visit.
You:	*What will you do?*
Child:	I will read my story to her.

Here's an example of a completed Guided Writing Practice.

<u>A Visit</u>
Today is Monday.
Grandma is coming to visit.
I will read my story to her.

After your Guided Writing Practice is written on paper, read it two times. First, read the passage aloud to your child in its entirety. Next, read the sentences together, pointing to each word and encouraging your child to read any words that she knows.

ACTIVITY SET 2:2

Guided Writing Practice

Sit down with your child for today's Guided Writing Practice. You may sit side-by-side and write on a tablet or you may use an easel with chart paper. Spend 5-10 minutes on this activity.

Write a short title at the top related to something that is happening today. You can also think about something that already happened earlier today. Discuss these events with your child and write several simple sentences. Here is one suggestion.

At a Glance: Activity Set 2:2

- Guided Writing Practice
- Pre-writing Activities: Nonfiction picture book or easy reader about a famous person

You: *Let's write a title for today's writing time. We'll call it "Today Is Special."*

You: *Let's look at our calendar. What day is today?*

Child: Today is Wednesday.

You: *What special thing happened today?*

Child: Eli lost his tooth today.

You: *What else can you tell me about today?*

Child: It is snowing.

Here's an example of a completed Guided Writing Practice.

<u>Today Is Special</u>
Today is Wednesday.
Eli lost his tooth today.
It is snowing.

After your Guided Writing Practice is written on paper, read it aloud two times (see Guided Writing Practice, Activity Set 2:1).

Pre-writing Activities

Advance Prep

Write the following words and phrases on lined paper and cut them into strips you and your child can manipulate on a flat desk top. Or, if you use a pocket chart, prepare the pocket chart for today's lesson. Use sentence strips to make the following words and sentence starters.

Write the title and each sentence starter on a separate strip:

I Am Special
I like to wear a
I like to ride in a
I like to eat a
And I love

Write one word each on separate sentence strips. *Be sure to include the period after each word:*

hat. coat. belt. car. truck. bus. cracker. grape. cookie.

Include one blank strip for your child's choice.

(Option: From a magazine, cut a picture of each of these nouns and glue a picture beside the word on each sentence strip.)

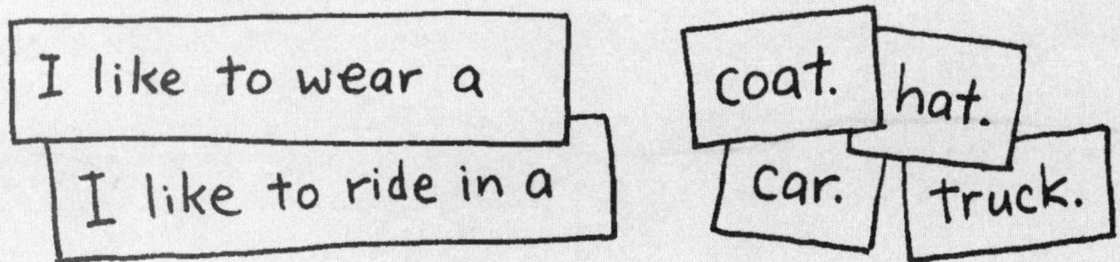

Arrange the strips on a desktop or prepare the pocket chart by placing the following strips in the chart:

I Am Special
I like to wear a
I like to ride in a
I like to eat a
And I love

Picture Book about a Famous Person

Read aloud a nonfiction picture book or easy reader about a famous person. When you are finished, ask, "What did you learn about that person? Why is he special?"

Characteristics of a Sentence

Read through the prepared sentence strips with your child, sentence by sentence.

1. Discuss how a sentence forms a complete thought. Show him that the sentence strips aren't complete thoughts until he adds the final word and punctuation.
2. Let him choose which word to place at the end of each sentence.
3. To complete the last sentence, your child should suggest the word you write on the blank strip.
4. When the sentences are all finished, read through them together one final time. Identify the title. Talk together about why each and every person is special and unique.

ACTIVITY SET 2:3

Guided Writing Practice

Write a short title at the top related to something that is happening today. Discuss these events with your child and write several simple sentences. Here is one suggestion.

You: *Let's write a title for today's writing time. We'll call it "Park Day."*

You: *Let's look at our calendar. What day is today?*

Child: Today is Friday.

You: *What are you wearing today?*

Child: I am wearing jeans and a red shirt.

You: *Where will we go today?*

Child: We will go to the park after school.

At a Glance: Activity Set 2:3

- Guided Writing Practice
- Brainstorming

Here's an example of a completed Guided Writing Practice.

Park Day
Today is Friday.
I am wearing jeans and a red shirt.
We will go to the park after school.

After your Guided Writing Practice is written on paper, read it aloud two times as you have done on previous days.

Brainstorming on Chart Paper

Ask your child why he is special. On a tablet or on chart paper, write down various responses.

Option: Take a picture of your child with a digital camera and print out the picture. Give him the picture to hold while you brainstorm together about why he's special.

ACTIVITY SET 2:4

Guided Writing Practice

Continue to focus Guided Writing Practice on something that is happening today. Sometimes you'll write about something special, but often you'll write about everyday activities. Begin by writing a short title at the top. Discuss these events with your child and write several simple sentences. Here is one suggestion.

At a Glance: Activity Set 2:4

- Guided Writing Practice
- The Writing Project
- Smaller Steps or Flying Higher

You: *Let's write a title for today's writing time.*
We'll call it "Tasty Meals."

You: *Let's look at the calendar. What day is today?*

Child: Today is Monday. Tuesday

You: *What did you eat for breakfast today?*

Child: I ate pancakes for breakfast. danish

You: *What would you like to eat for lunch?*

Child: I want a tuna sandwich for lunch. Sandwich

Here is an example of a completed Guided Writing Practice.

<u>Tasty Meals</u>
Today is Monday.
I ate pancakes for breakfast.
I want a tuna sandwich for lunch.

After your Guided Writing Practice is written on paper, read it aloud two times as you have done on previous days.

The Writing Project - About Me

Advance Prep

Cut construction paper into five 10-inch circles, the same size as the paper plate your child will use during Activity Set 2:7 (Publishing the Project, p. 46).

My name is ________.
There are ________ people in my family.

We live at ________. (address)
My phone number is ________.
I am special because ________.

Directions

1. Have your child write his name on the first page.
2. Encourage him to color a picture on each page and dictate the words for you to write in the blanks. (If your child is already an independent writer, he can write the words instead of dictating them to you.)
3. Use the ideas from your brainstorming session to complete the final sentence.

Smaller Steps - Memorizing Address and Phone Number

A younger learner may benefit from using this time to practice memorizing his address and phone number.

Flying Higher - More About Me

An advanced or accelerated student may want to add more pages, perhaps incorporating the ideas she will choose for her Activity Set Worksheet (favorite place, toy, or book). She might also add more pages about why she's special.

ACTIVITY SET 2:5

At a Glance: Activity Set 2:5

- Guided Writing Practice
- Editing and Revising

Guided Writing Practice

Write a short title at the top related to something that is happening today. Discuss these events with your child and write several simple sentences. Here is an example.

A New Nickel

You: *Let's look at the calendar. What day is today?*

Child: Today is Wednesday.

You: *Tell me something that happened today.*

Child: I found a nickel under the couch.

You: *What will you do with your nickel?*

Child: I will put my nickel in my money jar.

After your Guided Writing Practice is written on paper, read it aloud two times as you have done on previous days.

Editing and Revising

Sit down together with your child and review each of the five pages of her Writing Project.

1. Ask her to explain each picture to you. Check that her name is written correctly.
2. Discuss any changes that need to be made.
3. If your child is starting at a kindergarten level or is working at a pre-writing level, don't be too concerned with standard spelling. At this point, praise any attempt your child makes at writing independently. Standard spelling will come later after she learns to write all the letters correctly and begins writing words and sentences on her own.
4. Should your student need help writing her name, use this time to practice. With a young student, lightly write your child's name on a separate piece of paper. Have her practice tracing it until she is able to copy it on her own and eventually write it without a prompt. When ready, have her rewrite her name on the first page of the project.

ACTIVITY SET 2:6

Guided Writing Practice

Write a short title at the top related to something that is happening today. Discuss these events with your child and write several simple sentences. Here is an example.

Auntie's Birthday

You: *Let's look at the calendar. What day is today?*

Child: Today is Friday.

You: *What is special about today?*

Child: It's Auntie Lucy's birthday.

You: *What will you make for Auntie?*

Child: I will make a birthday card for her.

You: *What fun things will we do today?*

Child: We will go out for pizza and ice cream.

At a Glance: Activity Set 2:6

- Guided Writing Practice
- Activity Set Worksheet: "My Favorite Things"

After your Guided Writing Practice is written on paper, read it aloud two times as you have done on previous days.

Activity Set Worksheet: "My Favorite Things"

Use Lesson 2: "My Favorite Things" Activity Set Worksheet.

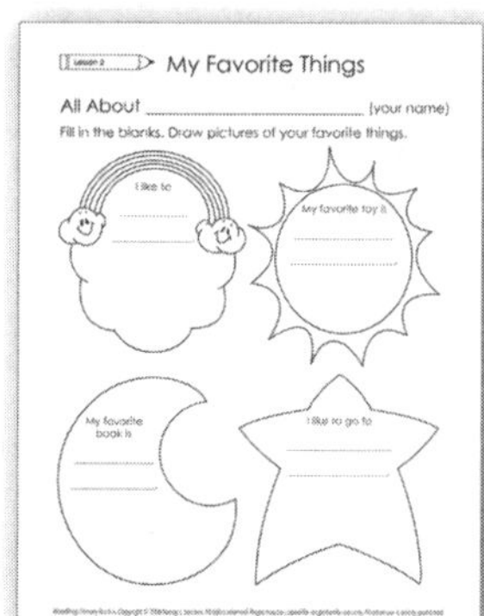

1. Help your student fill in the blanks and draw a picture of her favorite things.
2. On the back of the worksheet, encourage her to practice writing her name or one of the words she learned during this lesson.

ACTIVITY SET 2:7

Guided Writing Practice

Write a short title at the top related to something that is happening today. Discuss these events with your child and write several simple sentences. Here is an example.

Riding Bikes with Marco

You: *Let's look at the calendar. What day is today?*

Child: Today is Monday.

You: *What is going to happen today?*

Child: Marco is coming over to play.

You: *What will you do?*

Child: We will go outside and ride bikes.

At a Glance: Activity Set 2:7

- Guided Writing Practice
- Publishing the Project

After your Guided Writing Practice is written on paper, read it aloud two times as you have done on previous days.

Publishing the Project - Making a Paper Plate Face Book

To publish the Writing Project, assemble it into a book. Here's how.

1. Your child will use a 10-inch paper plate to make a picture of her face by decorating it with yarn, fabric scraps, and markers.
2. Place the pages of the writing project directly behind the paper plate and staple across the top.

ACTIVITY SET 2:8

Guided Writing Practice

Write a short title at the top related to something that is happening today. Discuss these events with your child and write several simple sentences. Here is an example.

A Daisy Field Trip

You: *Let's look at the calendar. What day is today?*

Child: Today is Wednesday.

You: *What are you wearing today?*

Child: I am wearing my Daisy uniform.

You: *What will you do today?*

Child: We will go on a field trip today.

You: *Where are you going?*

Child: We're going to the fire station.

At a Glance: Activity Set 2:8

- Guided Writing Practice
- Evaluating the Student's Work
- Want to Do More? (optional): Writing Across the Curriculum: Spotlight on Science
- Want to Do More? (optional): Computer Capers

After your Guided Writing Practice is written on paper, read it aloud two times as you have done on previous days.

Evaluating the Student's Work

Use the Primary Writing Skills Evaluation Chart for Lessons 1-5 to evaluate your student's work.

Want to Do More?

Writing Across the Curriculum: Spotlight on Science - I Am an Animal
Directions

1. Have your child pretend to be a certain animal. Read a nonfiction Internet article, magazine article, or picture book to discover interesting facts about this animal.
2. Your child will do the Writing Project again, this time describing what it would be like to be that animal. When finished, staple the pages to a paper plate and decorate the plate to resemble the animal's face. Here is a sample of the written science project:

   I am a __________. I live in a ___________. I like to eat ____________.
   I have _____________. I am special because _______________________.

   Example: I am a bear. I live in a cave. I like to eat berries. I have fur and claws. I am special because I can catch fish with my claws.

Computer Capers - Using Computers to Find Information

Directions

1. Use an encyclopedia software program on the computer or visit a kid-safe site on the Internet to find information about your child's favorite animal, sport, or other topic of interest. Print out this information and read it aloud for sharing.
2. Ask your child to share something special he learned about his favorite subject.

If you do not have encyclopedia software, consider these quality online sources instead:

- **Kids.gov** The official kids' portal for the U.S. government links to over 1,200 web pages from government agencies and educational organizations, all geared to the learning level and interest of kids. **www.kids.gov**
- **Great Web Sites for Kids (American Library Association)** Children's librarians have collected links to excellent sites for kids. **www.ala.org/greatsites**
- **kidsites.com** Each site is approved before a link is established. **www.kidsites.com**

Caution: Please supervise your child's computer time, especially her Internet use, so that you can guide her to sites with age-appropriate content.

Lesson 3: Choosing a Topic

Lesson Focus: Thinking of Ideas to Write About
Theme: My Favorite Things

Objectives

Your child will:

- Begin to recognize frequently-used letters and words.
- Learn to write down several possible ideas and choose one to write about.
- Discover there are many interesting and exciting ideas that can be used to write a story.
- Begin to understand most stories are about one main topic or idea.

Materials

Guided Writing Practice

- Tablet or chart paper and markers
- Manila file folder
- Several pictures from magazines or old calendars depicting different kinds of weather

Pre-writing Activities

- Picture book about something your child likes to think about or do
- Old children's magazines or toy catalogs
- Cardstock
- Craft sticks
- Scissors, glue, clear tape

Brainstorming

- Small file box with blank index cards
- Old magazines or catalogs
- Scissors, pencils, markers, tape, glue

The Writing Project

- Computer or copy paper, cut in half
- Pencils or markers

Publishing the Project

- 9- x12-inch construction paper or 12- x 12-inch scrapbooking paper (solid or patterned)
- Yarn
- Spring-type clothespins or paper clips
- Crayons or markers
- Scissors, glue

Want to Do More?

- Writing Across the Curriculum
  - ~ Several of your child's favorite books
  - ~ Same supplies as the Writing Project and Publishing the Project

ACTIVITY SET 3:1

Guided Writing Practice

At a Glance: Activity Set 3:1

- Guided Writing Practice

Advance Prep

Make a *Portable Word Bank* about seasons. Here's how:

1. Take advantage of the weather theme in the Guided Writing Practice in Lessons 3, 5, and 6 to help your child expand his season vocabulary. Whether the weather changes from day to day or stays the same, there can be plenty to say about it! Depending on where you live, summer weather can be *sunny, bright, warm, hot, dry, stormy*, or *clear*. Winter can be *mild, cool*, or *cold*, as well as *rainy, snowy*, or *windy*.
2. A *Portable Word Bank* of weather vocabulary for spring, summer, autumn (or fall), and winter will help your child choose just the right word (or words) for each day. Follow the directions on pp. 9-10 for working with your child to create a *Portable Word Bank* for grade-level season words.
3. Write Seasons on the folder tab. Glue several season or weather-related magazine pictures to the front of the folder (showing sun, clouds, snow, etc.) and write "Words about Seasons" as the title.
4. Store the folder in a file box.

You and your child are now familiar with Guided Writing Practice. Beginning with Lesson 3, you will start writing more predictable sentences by repeating the same four sentence starters each day of this lesson. This helps your child learn to recognize frequently-used letters and words.

Continue sharing the marker so your child writes any letters or words that she knows. Repeat this activity each day, spending no more than 5-10 minutes per session.

1. Using a marker, first write a title at the top of the page.
2. Write the first sentence starter, *Good morning*. Next, encourage your child to write her name, or any letters of her name, that she knows. If you have more than one child, write *Good morning, children*.

3. Write the second sentence starter, *Today is*. Ask your child to identify the correct day of the week to write on the paper.
4. Write the third sentence starter, *The weather is*. Talk about what kind of weather conditions you are experiencing today and decide together what to write down. Your *Portable Word Bank* of season words will be helpful. Sometimes your child might say, "The weather is sun," or "The weather is ice and snow." Because this is common for young children, it's okay to accept her word choices even though this is not the way we would normally "speak."
5. Conclude with the fourth sentence starter, *Today we will*. Since the theme of Lesson 3 is favorite things, discuss some favorite upcoming activities for the day and choose one to write about. Here are examples of what to write.

    <u>Our Cold Day</u>
    Good morning, Ruth.
    Today is Monday.
    The weather is clouds and rain.
    Today we will eat soup for lunch.

    <u>Friday Morning</u>
    Good morning, children!
    Today is Friday.
    The weather is sunny and warm.
    Today we will paint.

After your Guided Writing Practice is written on paper, read it two times. First, read the passage aloud to your child in its entirety. Next, read the sentences together, pointing to each word and encouraging your child to read any words that she knows.

ACTIVITY SET 3:2

Guided Writing Practice

Repeat the Guided Writing activity introduced in Activity Set 3:1.

> **At a Glance: Activity Set 3:2**
>
> - Guided Writing Practice
> - Pre-writing Activities: Picture book about a topic that interests your child

1. Using a marker, first write a title at the top of the page.
2. Write the first sentence starter, *Good morning*. Encourage your child to use the marker to write her name, or any letters of her name that she knows.
3. Write the second sentence starter, *Today is*. Ask your child to identify the correct day of the week to write on the paper.
4. Write the third sentence starter, *The weather is*. Talk about what kind of weather conditions you are experiencing today and decide together what to write down. Use the *Portable Word Bank* of season words to help with ideas.
5. Conclude with the fourth sentence starter, *Today we will*. Discuss some favorite upcoming activities for the day and choose one to write about. Here's an example.

    A Hot Day
    Good morning, Ryan.
    Today is Wednesday.
    The weather is hot.
    Today we will eat snow cones.

Read the completed Guided Writing Practice aloud two times.

- Read the passage aloud to your child in its entirety.
- Next, read the sentences together, pointing to each word and encouraging your child to read any words that she knows.

Pre-writing Activities

Advance Prep

Make several stick puppets about different things that interest your child such as a pony, ladybug, truck, or princess. To make each puppet, cut out a picture of the object from an old magazine or toy catalog. Glue the picture to a piece of cardstock. Tape a craft stick on the back.

Picture Book about a Topic That Interests Your Child

Read aloud a picture book about a topic that interests your child, such as going camping, visiting

Grandma's house, riding bikes, or playing with a friend. When you are finished, ask, "What was that book all about?" and "Why do you like to read about that topic?"

Stick Puppet Stories

1. Ask your child to hold one of the puppets and tell a short story about it. When his story is finished, use one of the puppets to tell your own story. Take turns making up simple stories using the different puppets.
2. When you finish, discuss how someone can make up a story about any topic he chooses.

ACTIVITY SET 3:3

Guided Writing Practice

Repeat the Guided Writing activity introduced in Activity Set 3:1.

Use a marker and write the following predictable sentence starters:

Title (Parent's choice)
Good morning, ____.
Today is ____. (Day of the week)
The weather is ____. (Or, *The weather is* ____ *and* ____.)
Today we will ____.

At a Glance: Activity Set 3:3

- Guided Writing Practice
- Brainstorming

After your Guided Writing Practice is written on paper, read it aloud two times as you have done on previous days.

Brainstorming - Making a Story Ideas File Box

Advance Prep

Create a small file box for potential topics of favorite things your child might like to write about. Label the file box *Story Ideas*. Tape or glue a small picture of a light bulb on the box. If you can't find a picture in a magazine, try searching **www.google.com**. Type "light bulb" in the search field and click "Images."

Make index cards to keep inside the box by gluing a small magazine or catalog picture on one side of the index card and writing the topic on the opposite side. For instance, make cards for topics similar to these: *baseball, horse, flower, doll, dog, bug, car, cake, pizza,* and *dinosaur.* Place at least 10 cards in the file box. Include several blank cards.

Directions for using the* Story Ideas File Box*:

1. During the brainstorming session, show the box of story ideas to your child. Take out the index cards. Look at the pictures together and read their labels. If you have a pocket chart, display the cards in the pockets. Ask your student to choose four cards (topics) he might like to write about.
2. If he wants to write about a topic that isn't in the file box, help him make a new index card by drawing or gluing a picture on the front and writing the label on the back.
3. Keep the file box at the Writing Center. In future lessons, when your student needs ideas or wants to write in his free time, encourage him to use the index cards in the file box to help spark his imagination. Periodically add new cards to the box.

ACTIVITY SET 3:4

Guided Writing Practice

Repeat the Guided Writing activity introduced in Activity Set 3:1.

Use a marker and write the following predictable sentence starters:

Title (Parent's choice)
Good morning, _____.
Today is _____. (Day of the week)
The weather is _____. (Or, *The weather is* _____ *and* _____.)
Today we will _____.

At a Glance: Activity Set 3:4

- Guided Writing Practice
- The Writing Project
- Smaller Steps or Flying Higher

After your Guided Writing Practice is written on paper, read it aloud two times as you have done on previous days.

The Writing Project - Favorite Things

Today your child will write about one of her favorite things.

Directions

1. Ask your child to choose one of the four index cards she selected during brainstorming. This will become her writing topic.
2. Have your child dictate a sentence or short story about the topic she picked. Write her response on a half sheet of paper. Or, she can write as much of the story as she is able to do herself.

Smaller Steps - Dictating a Story

As a younger child dictates, write down her story in large, bold letters. Help her track the letters as you write. Don't use tiny print, all-capital letters, or cursive handwriting.

Flying Higher - Adding Additional Story Elements

An advanced or accelerated student may enjoy picking three index cards and writing a story that includes all three elements. For example, if he chooses the *boy, ball,* and *pizza* index cards, he could write a story about a boy who eats pizza at a baseball game.

Alternatively, he might prefer to choose several index cards and write a different story for each topic. Use a separate sheet of paper for each story.

ACTIVITY SET 3:5

At a Glance: Activity Set 3:5

- Guided Writing Practice
- Editing and Revising

Guided Writing Practice

Repeat the Guided Writing activity introduced in Activity Set 3:1.

Use a marker and write the following predictable sentence starters:

> *Title* (Parent's choice)
> *Good morning,* _____.
> *Today is* _____. (Day of the week)
> *The weather is* _____. (Or, *The weather is* _____ *and* _____.)
> *Today we will* _____.

After your Guided Writing Practice is written on paper, read it aloud two times as you have done on previous days.

Editing and Revising

Sit down with your child and review the Writing Project story.

1. Ask her to explain the story to you. Read it aloud together.
2. Does the story make sense? Ask her if her story is about the topic she chose. If not, ask her what changes she could make to help the story make more sense.
3. If your child attempted to write any of the letters, words, or sentences on her own, praise her for her efforts. Don't worry too much about standard spelling at this point, but you can choose two or three misspelled words to sound out together and rewrite correctly.
4. If changes need to be made on the student's project, work together to make the final copy on a fresh half sheet of paper.

ACTIVITY SET 3:6

Guided Writing Practice

Repeat the Guided Writing activity introduced in Activity Set 3:1.

Use a marker and write the following predictable sentence starters:

Title (Parent's choice)
Good morning, _____.
Today is _____. (Day of the week)
The weather is _____. (Or, *The weather is* _____ *and* _____.)
Today we will _____.

> **At a Glance: Activity Set 3:6**
> - Guided Writing Practice
> - Activity Set Worksheet: "Bright Ideas"

After your Guided Writing Practice is written on paper, read it aloud two times as you have done on previous days.

Activity Set Worksheet: "Bright Ideas"

Use Lesson 3: "Bright Ideas" Activity Set Worksheet.

1. Have your child draw a different picture in each space to depict the topics he wants to write about. Next, help him label the picture by writing on the line.
2. On the back of the worksheet, he can practice further by writing independently about one of these four topics. A younger student can practice writing letters or words he knows how to spell.

In the future, if your child needs ideas to write about, have him fold a paper into four equal spaces. Just as he did on this worksheet, he can draw a picture in each space about four different topics that interest him. This helps spark ideas, especially for students who have trouble choosing a topic.

Use this method alternately with the *Story Ideas File Box* you created earlier in this lesson to show him there are many ways to come up with writing ideas.

ACTIVITY SET 3:7

Guided Writing Practice

Repeat the Guided Writing activity introduced in Activity Set 3:1.

Use a marker and write the following predictable sentence starters:

> *Title* (Parent's choice)
> *Good morning,* _____.
> *Today is* _____. (Day of the week)
> *The weather is* _____. (Or, *The weather is* _____ *and* _____.)
> *Today we will* _____.

At a Glance: Activity Set 3:7

- Guided Writing Practice
- Publishing the Project

After your Guided Writing Practice is written on paper, read it aloud two times as you have done on previous days.

Publishing the Project - Making a Story Clothesline

To publish the Writing Project, your child will hang his story on a clothesline. Here's how.

1. If there is room on the final copy, your child can illustrate his story.
2. Glue the story to a piece of construction paper cut in the shape of a pair of pants or a T-shirt.
3. Hang a simple yarn clothesline at the Writing Center to display your child's work. Use two spring-type clothespins or paperclips to hang the writing project on the clothesline.

If you have more than one child, or if your Flying Higher student wrote several stories, hang all the projects along the clothesline for a fun display of their creative writing efforts.

ACTIVITY SET 3:8

Guided Writing Practice

Repeat the Guided Writing activity introduced in Activity Set 3:1.

Use a marker and write the following predictable sentence starters:

Title (Parent's choice)
Good morning, _____.
Today is _____. (Day of the week)
The weather is _____. (Or, *The weather is* _____ *and* _____.)
Today we will _____.

At a Glance: Activity Set 3:8

- Guided Writing Practice
- Evaluating the Student's Work
- Want to Do More? (optional) Writing Across the Curriculum: Spotlight on Literature

After your Guided Writing Practice is written on paper, read it aloud two times as you have done on previous days.

Evaluating the Student's Work

Use the Primary Writing Skills Evaluation Chart for Lessons 1-5 to evaluate your student's work.

Want to Do More?

Writing Across the Curriculum: Spotlight on Literature - Retelling a Favorite Story

Directions

1. Do the writing project again. First browse through several of your child's favorite books. Ask him to describe the main idea or topic of each book. Invite him to choose one book you can read together.
2. Encourage your child to write or dictate a shortened version of the story in his very own words. Glue the story to a piece of construction paper cut in the shape of a T-shirt or a pair of pants. Clip to the clothesline displayed in your Writing Center.
3. During their free time, motivated students may want to create more projects to add to the clothesline.

Lesson 4:
The Main Idea

Lesson Focus: Selecting a Title
Theme: Friends

Objectives

Your child will:

- Determine the main idea and choose a title for several picture books.
- Practice completing predictable sentence starters.
- Write a short story about a friend and add a title to the story.
- Write several book titles about friends.

Materials

Guided Writing Practice

- Tablet or chart paper and markers

Pre-writing Activities

- Picture book about friends or friendship
- 3-5 picture books (any topic) your child has already read

Brainstorming

- Tablet or chart paper and markers

The Writing Project

- Brown construction paper
- Scissors
- Crayons or markers

Flying Higher

- Children's dictionary and thesaurus

Publishing the Project

- Crayons or markers
- Cookie jar or other container that works as a substitute
- Batch of cookies (either homemade or store-bought)

Want to Do More?

- Writing Across the Curriculum
    - ~ Writing paper
- Computer Capers
    - ~ Card-making software program

ACTIVITY SET 4:1

Guided Writing Practice

In the first three lessons, you chose the title for each day and then your child helped write the sentences. From now on, during most Guided Writing Practice sessions, you will:

At a Glance: Activity Set 4:1

- Guided Writing Practice

- Write predictable sentence starters.
- Encourage your child to finish each sentence with an original thought.
- Conclude by discussing various title possibilities. By adding the title last, it helps your child think of the main idea, an important concept for successful writing.

Write the following predictable sentence starters:

A friend is
Friends like to
Friends are special because

Discuss various options for ideas on how to complete each of the three sentences. Decide what to say. Then finish the sentences on the chart paper, sharing the marker so your child writes as many of the letters or words as she knows. Here is an example of how you can prompt your child.

You: *Let's think of some words that tell us about friends. I'll go first. A friend is funny. Now it's your turn.*

Child. A friend is happy.

You: *A friend is important.*

Child: A friend is kind.

You: *These are all great. Which one should we choose for today?*

Child: A friend is kind.

You: *Let's write that. A friend is kind. Here's the marker. Can you help me write the word* kind?

You: *What do friends like to do together?*

Child: Play games.

You: *Let's use complete thoughts. Friends like to play games together. Say that. "Friends like to play games together."*

Child: Friends like to play games together.

You: *Great. Let's write it down. Friends like to play games together. Can you help me with the marker?*

You: *Tell me—why are friends special?*

Child:	Because they share their toys?
You:	*Yes, that's a very important reason. Can you finish this sentence to make a complete thought? Friends are special because _____.*
Child:	Friends are special because they share their toys.
You:	*Good job. Now let's write that down. Friends are special because they share their toys.*

When finished, ask your child to help choose a title. Here's how.

1. Look for key words in each sentence.
   - Theme words: *friends* is the theme for this lesson
   - Action words: *play, share*
   - Naming words: *games, toys*
   - Describing words: *kind, special*
2. Choose two or more key words to form the title. Possible titles include:
   - Friends Like to Play
   - Friends Play Games
   - Friends Share Toys
   - Kind Friends
   - Friends Are Special
3. Write the title at the top.

Here is a sample of a completed Guided Writing Practice.

> <u>Kind Friends</u>
> A friend is kind.
> Friends like to play games together.
> Friends are special because they share their toys.

After your Guided Writing Practice is written on paper, read it two times. First, read the passage aloud to your child in its entirety. Next, read the sentences together, pointing to each word and encouraging your child to read any words that she knows.

ACTIVITY SET 4:2

Guided Writing Practice

Repeat the Guided Writing activity introduced in Activity Set 4:1.

> **At a Glance: Activity Set 4:2**
> - Guided Writing Practice
> - Pre-writing Activities: Picture book about friends or friendship

1. Write the first sentence starter, *A friend is*. Tell your child, "Let's think of words that can describe a friend." Prompt him with single-word answers such as *silly, playful, nice, happy, shy, helpful*. Alternatively, suggest short phrases such as *fun to be with, someone who likes me, in my neighborhood, like a brother/sister.*
2. Write the second sentence starter, *Friends like to*. Ask your child to think of more things that friends like to do. Write his answer on the paper.
3. Write the third sentence starter, *Friends are special because*. Talk about why friends are special and decide together what to write down.

When finished, ask your child to help choose a title, following the guidelines in Activity Set 4:1. Write the title at the top. Here is an example.

> Friends Love Each Other
> A friend is someone who comes to visit.
> Friends like to eat lunch together.
> Friends are special because they love each other.

After your Guided Writing Practice is written on paper, read it two times. First, read the passage aloud to your child in its entirety. Next, read the sentences together, pointing to each word and encouraging your child to read any words that she knows.

Pre-writing Activities

Picture Book about Friends or Friendship

Choose a picture book about friends or friendship to read to your child.

1. Do not show him the title, but begin reading the story.
2. After the story is finished, ask him to suggest titles for the book. Then show him the actual title of the book.
3. Explain how the title gives the reader a clue about the main idea of the story.

Gather a selection of 3-5 picture books your child has already read.

1. Without showing the title, hold up one of the open books and give a short summary of it.
2. Ask your child to suggest possible titles, including the actual one.
3. Discuss why each suggestion would or would not give an adequate clue about the main idea of the story.
4. Repeat this exercise with the remaining books.

ACTIVITY SET 4:3

Guided Writing Practice

For the rest of Lesson 4, repeat the Guided Writing activity introduced in Activity Set 4:1. Write the following predictable sentence starters:

> *A friend is* (See Activity Set 4:2 for prompt ideas.)
> *Friends like to*
> *Friends are special because*

At a Glance: Activity Set 4:3

- Guided Writing Practice
- Brainstorming

When finished, ask your child to help choose a title, following the guidelines in Activity Set 4:1. Write the title at the top. Here is an example.

> A Soccer Friend
> A friend is on my soccer team.
> Friends like to share the ball.
> Friends are special because they take turns.

After your Guided Writing Practice is written on paper, read it aloud two times as you have done on previous days.

Brainstorming - Choosing Describing Words and Titles

1. Ask your student to think of titles for stories about friends. Write the ideas at the top of a piece of paper. Possible suggestions include: *I Am a Friend, I Like Friends, Pets Are Friends, Grandpa Is My Friend, My Friend Ben, Friends Are Fun, Friends on My Street.*
2. At the bottom of the paper, brainstorm a list of words that describe friends. Possible suggestions include: *helpful, kind, fun, silly, happy, nice, friendly, understanding, caring, loving, forgiving, and generous.*

ACTIVITY SET 4:4

Guided Writing Practice

Write the following predictable sentence starters:

> *A friend is* _____. (See Activity Set 4:2 Guided Writing Practice for prompt ideas.)
> *Friends like to* _____.
> *Friends are special because* _____.

At a Glance: Activity Set 4:4

- Guided Writing Practice
- The Writing Project
- Smaller Steps or Flying Higher

When finished, ask your child to help choose a title, following the guidelines in Activity Set 4:1. Write the title at the top.

After your Guided Writing Practice is written on paper, read it aloud two times as you have done on previous days.

The Writing Project - I Am a Friend

Advance Prep

- Out of brown construction paper, cut a 5-inch circle to represent a cookie.
- Allowing room at the top for a title, on the paper cookie write the sentence:

I am a _____ friend because ________________________.

Directions

1. Give your child the paper cookie.
2. Help your child choose a word from the brainstorming list to describe the kind of friend she is. According to her skill level, have her dictate or write the word on the cookie and complete the sentence.
3. Have her choose a title to write above the sentence, using the brainstorming list as a reference. Choosing a title for a sentence helps her focus quickly on the main idea.
4. Read over the title and the sentence together.

Smaller Steps - Helping the Pre-writer

Write the word and complete the sentence lightly in pencil for a younger child. Encourage him to trace over each letter with a crayon.

Flying Higher - Introducing the Dictionary and Thesaurus

Use a children's dictionary with an advanced or accelerated student to look up the meaning of unfamiliar words. Introduce a thesaurus to him and find new words to describe friends.

ACTIVITY SET 4:5

Guided Writing Practice

Write the following predictable sentence starters:

> *A friend is* _____. (See Activity Set 4:2 Guided Writing Practice for prompt ideas.)
> *Friends like to* _____.
> *Friends are special because* _____.

At a Glance: Activity Set 4:5

- Guided Writing Practice
- Editing and Revising

When finished, ask your child to help choose a title, following the guidelines in Activity Set 4:1. Write the title at the top.

After your Guided Writing Practice is written on paper, read it aloud two times as you have done on previous days.

Editing and Revising

Sit down together with your child and her Writing Project story.

1. Review the sentence and title. Ask, "Does the title give a clue about the main idea?" If not, discuss ideas for a better title.
2. If your child attempted to write any of the letters or words herself, praise her for her efforts. Do not worry too much about standard spelling at this point, but you can choose one or two misspelled words to sound out together and rewrite correctly.
3. Have your child make corrections to the title at the top, or make a new cookie, rewriting the title and sentence on it.

ACTIVITY SET 4:6

Guided Writing Practice

Write the following predictable sentence starters:

> *A friend is* _____. (See Activity Set 4:2 Guided Writing Practice for prompt ideas.)
> *Friends like to* _____.
> *Friends are special because* _____.

At a Glance: Activity Set 4:6

- Guided Writing Practice
- Activity Set Worksheet: "Book Titles for Friends"

When finished, ask your child to help choose a title, following the guidelines in Activity Set 4:1. Write the title at the top.

After your Guided Writing Practice is written on paper, read it aloud two times as you have done on previous days.

Activity Set Worksheet: "Book Titles for Friends"

Use Lesson 4: "Book Titles for Friends" Activity Set Worksheet.

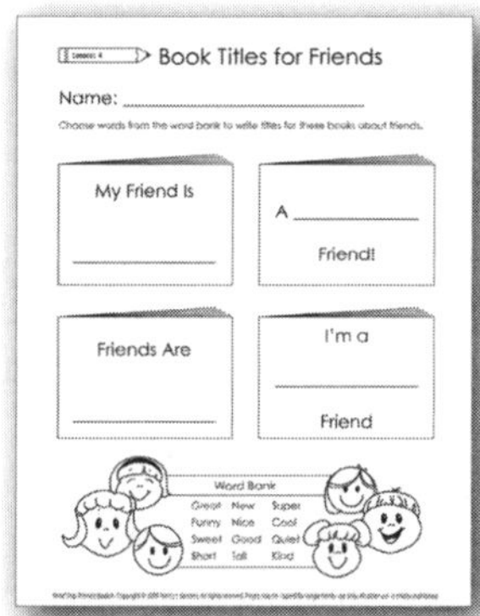

Book Titles for Friends

Name: ____________________

Choose words from the word bank to write titles for these books about friends.

My Friend Is ____________

A ____________ Friend!

Friends Are ____________

I'm a ____________ Friend

Word Bank

Great	New	Super
Funny	Nice	Cool
Sweet	Good	Quiet
Short	Tall	Kind

1. Have your child use the words from the word bank to fill in the blanks.
2. On the back of the page, your child can draw a picture of himself with a friend and write a simple story about what they are doing together.
3. After the story is written, help your child choose a title to write at the top.

ACTIVITY SET 4:7

Guided Writing Practice

Write the following predictable sentence starters:

> *A friend is* _____. (See Activity Set 4:2 Guided Writing Practice for prompt ideas.)
> *Friends like to* _____.
> *Friends are special because* _____.

At a Glance: Activity Set 4:7

- Guided Writing Practice
- Publishing the Project

When finished, ask your child to help choose a title, following the guidelines in Activity Set 4:1. Write the title at the top.

After your Guided Writing Practice is written on paper, read it aloud two times as you have done on previous days.

Publishing the Project - Making Paper "Friendship" Cookies

To publish the Writing Project, your child will finish making the paper cookies he worked on during Activity Set 4:4.

1. Have the child decorate the other side of the cookie to make it look like a chocolate chip cookie or other cookie of his choice.
2. If you are only teaching one or two students, instruct each child to make several more cookies. Each cookie should describe a different attribute the child has that makes him a good friend.
3. Add a title to the top. Be sure the child's name is written on each cookie.
4. Put all the cookies in a cookie jar. Use a real cookie jar or other similar container.

Enjoy a Tasty Treat

Bring in a tray of real cookies or make a batch of cookies with your child. If you have one student or a small class, share a couple of cookies together while you take turns choosing paper cookies out of the jar and reading them aloud.

If you're teaching a group of children, invite each student to choose one paper cookie from the jar and read it aloud. Then enjoy eating the real cookies together!

ACTIVITY SET 4:8

Guided Writing Practice

Write the following predictable sentence starters:

> *A friend is* ____. (See Activity Set 4:2 Guided Writing Practice for prompt ideas.)
> *Friends like to* ____.
> *Friends are special because* ____.

When finished, ask your child to help choose a title, following the guidelines in Activity Set 4:1. Write the title at the top.

After your Guided Writing Practice is written on paper, read it aloud two times as you have done on previous days.

At a Glance: Activity Set 4:8

- Guided Writing Practice
- Evaluating the Student's Work
- Want to Do More? (optional) Writing Across the Curriculum: Spotlight on Physical Fitness
- Want to Do More? (optional) Computer Capers

Evaluating the Student's Work

Use the Primary Writing Skills Evaluation Chart for Lessons 1-5 to evaluate your student's work.

Want to Do More?

Writing Across the Curriculum: Spotlight on Physical Fitness - A Motion Song
Directions

1. Brainstorm a list of actions friends make, such as waving hello, giving a hug, or skipping and playing.
2. If you are teaching just one or two students, stand together. If you have a large class, gather in a circle, asking a volunteer to stand in the middle. Sing the following words to the tune of "Here We Go Round the Mulberry Bush." Take turns completing the rhyme describing actions friends make, and demonstrating the motions.

   This is the way we _____, _____, _____.
   This is the way we _____ *while playing with our friends.*

   Here are samples of verses to sing:

   This is the way we give a hug, give a hug, give a hug.
   This is the way we give a hug while playing with our friends.

   This is the way we jump and play, jump and play, jump and play.
   This is the way we jump and play while playing with our friends.

   This is the way we share our toys, share our toys, share our toys.
   This is the way we share our toys while playing with our friends.

3. When finished, help your child write out one or more verses of the song, describing what she likes to do the most while playing with her friends. Add a title that sums up the main idea.

Computer Capers - Making a Greeting Card

Help your child use a card-making program to make a card for a special friend. Here's how.

1. On the inside, write a message thanking her for being a friend. Referring to the brainstorming list, choose several words to describe her as a friend.
2. Write a title on the front.
3. Add illustrations and print out the card.
4. Encourage your child to sign it and give it to his friend.

Here is a sample card.

Front of card:
My Best Friend

Inside of card:

Thank you for being my friend.
You are cheerful, kind, and happy.
Love, Benjamin

Lesson 5: Story Structure

Lesson Focus: Constructing a Beginning, Middle, and End
Theme: Trains

Objectives

Your child will:

- Think of an introduction, a body, and a closing to the story he will compose.
- Organize ideas by using a simple graphic organizer.
- Make a word bank of words to choose from when writing his story.
- Create a five-sentence story.

Materials

Guided Writing Practice

- Tablet or chart paper and markers
- *Portable Word Bank* of season words

Pre-writing Activities

- Picture book about a train
- Manila file folder
- Picture of a train
- Markers, glue

Brainstorming

- Tablet or chart paper and markers

The Writing Project

- Grade-level writing paper
- Pencils or markers

Publishing the Project

- 2 pages from the Activity Set Worksheet Pack—Lesson 5: "My Story Train" (photocopy extra pages if your child will do the Flying Higher activity)
- 12- x 18-inch piece of construction paper
- Markers or crayons
- Tape, glue

Want to Do More?

- Writing Across the Curriculum
  - ~ Construction or scrapbooking paper, including gold or yellow

~ Markers or crayons
~ Stapler or tape
~ Small self-closing baggies

ACTIVITY SET 5:1

Guided Writing Practice

Write the following predictable sentence starters:

> *Today is*
> *The season is*
> *The weather is*
> *We like today because*
> *Today will be*

At a Glance: Activity Set 5:1

- Guided Writing Practice

Discuss various options for completing each of the five sentences, using the *Portable Word Bank* of season words you made in Activity Set 3:1.

Explain that the first sentence is the beginning and needs to introduce the idea. Point out that the next three sentences are the middle and present important information. Explain that the last sentence brings everything to an end.

Share the marker so he writes as many of the letters or words as he knows how. When the sentences are finished, ask your child to help choose a title. Write the title at the top. Here is a sample of a completed Guided Writing Practice.

> A Visit from Grandpa Jim
> Today is Monday.
> The season is summer.
> The weather is sunny.
> We like today because Grandpa Jim is coming over.
> Today will be fun.

After your Guided Writing Practice is written on paper, read it two times. First, read the passage aloud to your child in its entirety. Next, read the sentences together, pointing to each word and encouraging your child to read any words that he knows.

You will use the same predictable sentence starters every day of Lesson 5. Even if this exercise seems dry or dull to you, remember that young children thrive on repetition and predictability!

ACTIVITY SET 5:2

Guided Writing Practice

For the rest of Lesson 5, repeat the Guided Writing activity introduced in Activity Set 5:1. Write the following predictable sentence starters:

Today is
The season is
The weather is
We like today because
Today will be

At a Glance: Activity Set 5:2

- Guided Writing Practice
- Pre-writing Activities: Picture book about trains

Discuss various options for completing each of the five sentences, using the *Portable Word Bank* of season words. Share the marker so she writes as many of the letters or words as she knows how.

Review story structure with your child:

1. The first sentence is the beginning and needs to introduce the idea.
2. The next three sentences are the middle and present important information.
3. The last sentence brings everything to an end.

When the sentences are finished, ask your child to help choose a title. Write the title at the top. Example:

<u>Art Day</u>
Today is Tuesday.
The season is summer.
The weather is warm.
We like today because it is art day.
Today will be a messy painting day.

After your Guided Writing Practice is written on paper, read it aloud two times (see Activity Set 5:1).

Pre-writing Activities

Picture Book about Trains

Choose a picture book about trains to read to your child. When finished, ask her to identify the beginning, the middle, and the end of the story.

Portable Word Bank

If you made a *Portable Word Bank* of season words in Activity Set 3:1, you have already discovered that this is a great tool to help young students develop their reading and writing vocabulary. Throughout the upcoming lessons of WriteShop Primary, you will make many theme-related *Portable Word Banks*. Your child can use them as a handy reference while she writes.

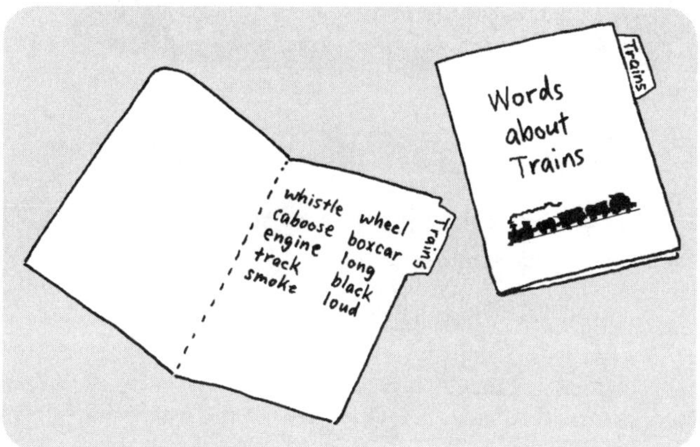

Make a *Portable Word Bank* of vocabulary words your child can use to write her train story. Here's how:

1. Glue a picture of a train on the front of a manila file folder. (Find a picture in an old calendar, toy catalog, or online.)
2. On the front of the file folder, write: *Words about Trains*
3. Together with your child, think of words that relate to trains, such as *big, loud, long, black, smoke, track, whistle, boxcar, caboose*, and *engine*. Write these words on the inside of the file folder. Try to use mostly grade-level words. For example, a second grader might know the word *boxcar*, but a kindergartener might not. Still, a few more advanced words are all right to include as well.
4. For handy storage, label the tab with the title "Trains" and store the folder in a file box.
5. Your child should refer to this *Portable Word Bank* as she writes. She may add more words to the list as she thinks of them.
6. As her collection of *Portable Word Banks* grows, encourage your child to use these folders for future writing assignments.

ACTIVITY SET 5:3

Guided Writing Practice

For the rest of Lesson 5, repeat the Guided Writing activity introduced in Activity Set 5:1. Write the following predictable sentence starters:

Today is
The season is
The weather is
We like today because
Today will be

At a Glance: Activity Set 5:3

- Guided Writing Practice
- Brainstorming

Talk about ways to complete each of the five sentences, using the *Portable Word Bank* of season words. Share the marker so he writes as many of the letters or words as he knows how.

When the sentences are finished, ask your child to help choose a title. Write the title at the top. Here is a sample of a completed Guided Writing Practice.

<u>Playing in the Leaves</u>
Today is Friday.
The season is fall.
The weather is clear and cool.
We like today because we get to play in the leaves.
Today will be a raking day.

After your Guided Writing Practice is written on paper, read it aloud two times as you have done on previous days.

Brainstorming - Making a Simple Graphic Organizer

Directions

1. Make a simple graphic organizer on chart paper to list ideas for the introduction, body, and closing of a story. Label the graphic organizer as follows, leaving spaces for writing as you brainstorm together.

   Title:
   Beginning:
   Middle:
   End:

2. Sit with your child and ask him to think of story ideas about trains. Ask questions such as, "What could happen on a train full of zoo animals?" or "What could happen on a train ride through the mountains?"

3. As you discuss the ideas together for one story, talk about what might happen at the beginning of the story, in the middle, and at the end. Discuss potential titles. Write these ideas down on your graphic organizer.
4. If your child suggests different story ideas, repeat the brainstorming activity on a separate piece of paper for each idea.

ACTIVITY SET 5:4

At a Glance: Activity Set 5:4

- Guided Writing Practice
- The Writing Project
- Smaller Steps or Flying Higher

Guided Writing Practice

Write the following predictable sentence starters:

Today is
The season is
The weather is
We like today because
Today will be

Discuss various options for completing each of the five sentences, following the Activity Set 5:1 model and using the *Portable Word Bank* of season words. When the sentences are finished, ask your child to help choose a title. Write the title at the top. Here is a sample of a completed Guided Writing Practice.

A Cozy Day
Today is Thursday.
The season is winter.
The weather is gray and rainy.
We like today because Mom made waffles for breakfast.
Today will be a good day to read books.

After your Guided Writing Practice is written on paper, read it aloud two times as you have done on previous days.

The Writing Project - A Train Story

Directions

1. For the writing project, your child will write a five-sentence story about a train. (He may dictate to you or write as much as he can independently.)
2. Ask him to choose a story idea from one of the Brainstorming chart papers. On a piece of writing paper, have him write one sentence to introduce the story. Then have him write the three middle sentences telling different things that happen in the story. This forms the body of his composition. Finally, have him write one sentence to draw the story to an end. Do not write a paragraph. Instead, write the sentences in list form, as in the examples below. After the story is written down, help your child choose a title. Here are three examples of completed stories.

   My Train
   Once there was a train that could fly.
   It flew to the zoo.
   It flew to the moon.
   It flew to my house.
   Then it stayed with me forever.

My Train Trip
Last year I took a trip on a train.
I saw cities.
I saw mountains.
I saw rivers.
This summer I want to go again.

Fairy Tale Train
Once upon a time, the three little pigs had a train.
The pigs put straw, sticks, and bricks on the train.
The pigs built their houses on the train.
A wolf came and tried to blow down their houses.
But the pigs rode the train far away.

Smaller Steps - Using Sentence Starters

A younger learner may feel frustrated trying to think of sentences to form the body of her story. Offer sentence starters, using the ideas from your brainstorming session to prompt ideas. Encourage your child to complete the sentence starters in her own words.

Flying Higher - Writing a Longer Story

An advanced or accelerated learner may want to add more sentences to form the body of a longer story. If so, when you publish the project, be sure to first photocopy extra boxcars for her to use from the "My Story Train" Activity Set Worksheets. Each sentence from the body of her story will be written on its own boxcar.

ACTIVITY SET 5:5

Guided Writing Practice

Write the following predictable sentence starters:

Today is
The season is
The weather is
We like today because
Today will be

> **At a Glance: Activity Set 5:5**
> - Guided Writing Practice
> - Editing and Revising

Discuss various options for completing each of the five sentences, following the Activity Set 5:1 model and using the *Portable Word Bank* of season words. When the sentences are finished, ask your child to help choose a title. Write the title at the top.

After your Guided Writing Practice is written on paper, read it aloud two times as you have done on previous days.

Editing and Revising

1. Sit down with your child and his Writing Project story. Read the train story together.
2. Discuss the structure of the story. Ask, "Does your story have a beginning, a middle, and an end?" "Does the title express the main idea or tell what the story is going to be about?" If not, discuss ideas for improvement.
3. Use this time to help your child write down the changes to his story.

ACTIVITY SET 5:6

Guided Writing Practice

Write the following predictable sentence starters:

Today is
The season is
The weather is
We like today because
Today will be

At a Glance: Activity Set 5:6

- Guided Writing Practice
- Activity Set Worksheet: "My Story Train"

Discuss various options for completing each of the five sentences, following the Activity Set 5:1 model and using the *Portable Word Bank* of season words. When the sentences are finished, ask your child to help choose a title. Write the title at the top.

After your Guided Writing Practice is written on paper, read it aloud two times as you have done on previous days.

Activity Set Worksheet: "My Story Train"

Use Lesson 5: "My Story Train" Activity Set Worksheets (two pages) to help your child write the final copy of her Writing Project story.

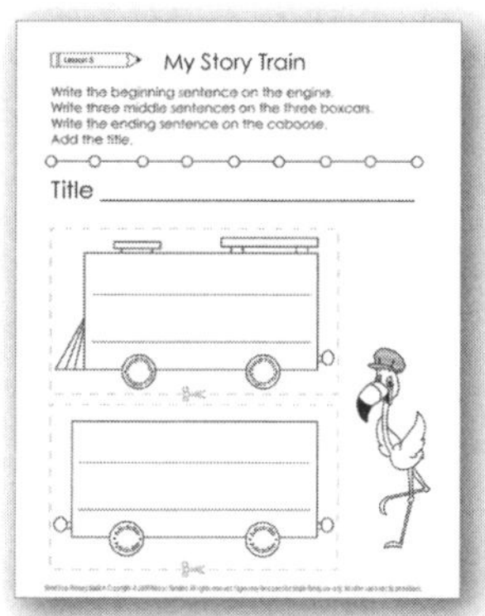

1. Write the title at the top of the first page.
2. Write the beginning sentence on the picture of the train engine, the three middle sentences on the three boxcars, and the ending sentence on the caboose.

ACTIVITY SET 5:7

Guided Writing Practice

Write the following predictable sentence starters:

Today is
The season is
The weather is
We like today because
Today will be

At a Glance: Activity Set 5:7

- Guided Writing Practice
- Publishing the Project

Discuss various options for completing each of the five sentences, following the Activity Set 5:1 model and using the *Portable Word Bank* of season words. When the sentences are finished, ask your child to help choose a title. Write the title at the top.

After your Guided Writing Practice is written on paper, read it aloud two times as you have done on previous days.

Publishing the Project - Making a Train Storybook

Advance Prep

Cut a 12- x 18-inch piece of construction paper in half lengthwise. Without overlapping the edges, tape the two pieces of paper end to end to form one long strip. Make six equal sections by accordion-folding the strip.

To publish his project, your child will make a small folded paper "book" to share his story. Here's how.

1. Using both Activity Set Worksheets of Lesson 5: "My Story Train," cut along the dashed lines as indicated to cut out the train engine, three boxcars, and caboose.
2. Open the accordion-folded paper strip to lie flat on a desk. On the first section of the construction paper strip, help your child write the title and his name. On the second section, have him glue the train engine. On the next three sections, glue the boxcars, putting the sentences in correct order. Glue the caboose on the last section.
3. Fold the accordion strip up to carry or store. Open it and read the story to a friend, a parent, or a sibling.

ACTIVITY SET 5:8

Guided Writing Practice

Write the following predictable sentence starters:

> *Today is*
> *The season is*
> *The weather is*
> *We like today because*
> *Today will be*

At a Glance: Activity Set 5:8

- Guided Writing Practice
- Evaluating the Student's Work
- Want to Do More? (optional) Writing Across the Curriculum: Spotlight on Language Arts

Discuss various options for completing each of the five sentences, following the Activity Set 5:1 model and using the *Portable Word Bank* of season words. When the sentences are finished, ask your child to help choose a title. Write the title at the top.

After your Guided Writing Practice is written on paper, read it aloud two times as you have done on previous days.

Evaluating the Student's Work

Use the Primary Writing Skills Evaluation Chart for Lessons 1-5 to evaluate your student's work.

Want to Do More?

Writing Across the Curriculum: Spotlight on Language Arts - Vocabulary: Making Paper Coins and a Purse or Wallet

It's important to encourage each step primary students take. As your child starts learning to write sight words, high-frequency words, or other vocabulary, she can keep track of her progress by adding golden coins to a paper wallet or purse. Here's how:

1. Cut a stack of 3-inch circles from gold or yellow construction or scrapbooking paper to represent gold coins. Place these in a self-closing plastic sandwich bag in your portable writing center, or place in a small basket at the permanent writing center.
2. Help your child make a wallet or purse by folding an 9- x 12-inch piece of construction or scrapbooking paper in half to form a 4½ - x 12-inch pocket. Tape or staple the sides together and decorate the pocket to resemble a purse or wallet.
3. When she learns how to spell and write a word correctly, have her write this word on a gold coin and place it inside her paper wallet or purse.

   Beginning Writers
   As your child learns how to write her name (or basic words such as *I, a, and, or, the*) have her write down each word on separate coins and slip them into her purse or wallet.

Older or Advanced Writers

More advanced students who already have a basic writing vocabulary can expand it by writing more difficult or challenging words on their coins.

4. During upcoming lessons, continue to add new coins as she learns how to write new words. As you watch her collection of gold coins grow, you'll see her confidence and independent writing skills grow, too.

Lesson 6: Punctuation

Lesson Focus: Using a Period at the End of a Sentence
Theme: Colors

Objectives

Your child will:

- Track words while reading a sentence.
- Learn that every sentence has an end mark.
- Identify a period at the end of a sentence.
- Learn that the punctuation mark at the end of a sentence is followed by a capital letter at the beginning of the next sentence.
- Practice identifying, reading, writing, and spelling various color words.

Materials

Guided Writing Practice

- Pointers (materials will vary; for ideas see p. 89 Guided Writing Practice, Advance Prep)
- Tablet or chart paper and markers
- *Portable Word Bank* of season words
- Small (1/4- or 1/2-inch) round stickers (either solid color or with a fun decoration)
- Star-shaped stickers (1/4- or 1/2-inch)

Pre-writing Activities

- Picture book about colors (must contain complete sentences and not just individual words)
- Writing paper or pocket chart with prepared sentence strips
- Markers, scissors, old catalogs or magazines, glue

Brainstorming

- Tablet or chart paper and markers
- Manila file folder
- Picture of a rainbow
- Construction paper in a variety of colors
- Markers, scissors, glue

The Writing Project

- Grade-level writing paper
- Pencils or markers
- Small round stickers (1/4- or 1/2-inch)
- Star-shaped stickers (1/4- or 1/2-inch)

Activity Set Worksheet

- Crayons or markers
- Scissors, glue

Publishing the Project

- Dinner-sized white paper plate
- Cardboard, poster board, or tagboard
- Scissors, stapler, glue
- Crayons, markers, or paint

Want to Do More?

- Writing Across the Curriculum
    - ~ Paintings of a famous artist from a book, Internet, or art collection. (If you decide to visit an art museum for this activity, be sure to stop at the gift shop. Help your child choose a postcard of a favorite painting to bring home for the actual writing portion of Want to Do More?)
    - ~ Grade-level writing paper
    - ~ Markers or pencils
    - ~ Small round stickers (1/4- or 1/2-inch)
    - ~ Star-shaped stickers (1/4- or 1/2-inch)

ACTIVITY SET 6:1

Guided Writing Practice

At a Glance: Activity Set 6:1

- Guided Writing Practice

Advance Prep

Collect or make at least five pointers to keep at your writing center. If you normally sit side-by-side during the Guided Writing activity, a smaller 8- to 12-inch pointer works nicely. If you use a large easel, choose a longer pointer. Each day, your child may select a different pointer to use.

- Pick ready-made objects such as a long candy cane, fancy ruler, paint brush, chopstick, toy wand, candle, tall decorative pencil, twig, or Pixy Stix®.
- A wiggly learner might enjoy searching the house for a special pointer.
- Ready-made objects tend to be shorter than 12 inches. If you find that you need longer pointers, plan to make them instead. You can make a fun pointer from a dowel rod with a small toy or colorful pencil-topper glued to one end.

Pointers are fun and educational! They help children track words better, strengthening reading and writing skills. Now that your child has become very familiar with how Guided Writing Practice works, take turns using the pointers as you read the completed sentences together.

Sit side-by-side with your child and write on a tablet, or use an easel with chart paper. Spend no more than 5-10 minutes on this activity. Use a marker and write the following predictable sentence starters:

Today is
The season is
The weather is
Today is a ______ day because (insert a color word in the blank)
Today will be

Discuss various options for ideas on how to complete each of the five sentences. For example, to find out more about today's weather, ask your child to look out the window or open the front door. If you made a *Portable Word Bank* of season words during Activity Set 3:1, pull it out again to use during Lesson 6.

Remind your child that stories have a beginning, a middle, and an end. The beginning introduces the story to the reader. The middle is the body, or content, of the story. The end draws the story to a close.

Share the marker so the child writes as many of the letters or words as she knows how. Make sure she fills in the blank with a color word and finishes the sentence accordingly. Here's one idea of how to do this.

You:	*I think today is a green day because I'm going to pull some weeds in the garden. What color do YOU think today is?*
Child:	I don't know.
You:	*OK, let's see if I can help. Are you doing something special this afternoon?*
Child:	We're going swimming.
You:	*Well, what color is our wading pool?*
Child:	Blue.
You:	*Then could today be a blue day?*
Child:	Yes…
You:	*OK. Today is a blue day because…why?*
Child:	Today is a blue day because we're going swimming in our pool?
You:	*Super! Yes! Let's write that down. Today is a blue day because we're going swimming in our pool. Help me write some of these words.*

When the sentences are finished, ask your child to help choose a title that includes her color word. Write the title at the top. Here is a sample of a completed Guided Writing Practice.

A Cool Blue Pool
Today is Monday.
The season is summer.
The weather is smoggy and hot.
Today is a blue day because we're going swimming in our pool.
Today will be a splashy swim day.

Help your child identify periods and capital letters. Here's how.

1. Using the pointer yourself, read over the sentences together. At the end of each sentence, point to the period and pause before going on.
2. When you have finished reading, ask your child what she sees at the end of every sentence. Ask her why she thinks those marks are there. Next, point to all the periods and explain that this special sign, called a period, tells the reader the sentence has come to an end.
3. Ask the child what she notices about the first word of each sentence. Help her recognize that each sentence starts with a capital letter. Discuss how each period is always followed by a capital letter.
4. Hand the pointer to your child. Ask her to point to each word as you read the sentences together again. Tell her to stop at the end of each sentence and point to the period. Hold her hand and guide her along if she is unable to track each word on her own.
5. Next, place a small round sticker over the period of the first sentence. Use solid-colored stickers or round stickers with a smiley face or other fun decoration.

6. Ask your child to locate each of the other periods and put a sticker over each one.
7. Count the number of sentences you have. Count the number of periods. Compare these numbers with your child and note again that each sentence has an end mark.
8. Ask your child to locate the capital letter at the beginning of each sentence and place a star-shaped sticker above it.

You will use the same predictable sentence starters every day of Lesson 6.

ACTIVITY SET 6:2

Guided Writing Practice

Write the following predictable sentence starters:

Today is
The season is
The weather is
Today is a ______ day because (insert a color word in the blank)
Today will be

> **At a Glance: Activity Set 6:2**
> - Guided Writing Practice
> - Pre-writing Activities: Picture book about colors

Discuss various options for ideas on how to complete each of the five sentences. If you made a *Portable Word Bank* of season words, pull it out to use again. Make sure your child fills in the blank with a color word.

When the sentences are finished, ask him to help choose a title that includes his color word. Write the title at the top. Here is a sample of a completed Guided Writing Practice.

A Black Cloud Day
Today is Tuesday.
The season is fall.
The weather is cloudy and rainy.
Today is a black day because the clouds are big and dark.
Today will be a dark, wet day.

Use the pointer yourself as you read over the sentences together. Review the following with your child.

- A period tells the reader the sentence has come to an end.
- A period is always followed by a capital letter.

Follow the same steps as in Guided Writing Practice, Activity Set 6:1. Here's how.

1. Hand the pointer to your child.
2. Ask him to point to each word as you read the sentences together again. Hold his hand and guide him along if he is unable to track each word on his own.
3. Tell him to stop at the end of each sentence and point to the period.
4. Place a small round sticker over the period of the first sentence.
5. Ask your child to locate each of the other periods and put a sticker over each one.
6. Count the number of sentences you have. Count the number of periods. Compare these numbers with your child and note again that each sentence has an end mark.

7. Ask your child to locate the capital letter at the beginning of each sentence and place a star-shaped sticker above it.

Pre-writing Activities

Advance Prep

If you are not using a Pocket Chart, write the following words and phrases on lined paper and cut them into strips that you and your child can manipulate on a flat surface.

If you are using a Pocket Chart, ready it for today's lesson by preparing the "Fun with Colors" action poem. Use 9 sentence strips to write out the title and 8 sentences. Put each of the strips in order on a tabletop or place one sentence strip in each line of the pocket chart. (DO NOT write a period at the end of the sentences.)

Fun with Colors
Red truck, red truck, drive around
Green frog, green frog, hop up and down
Yellow star, yellow star, dance in the sky
Blue ball, blue ball, bounce up high
Orange cat, orange cat, say meow
Black bear, black bear, take a bow
Purple car, purple car, zoom and roar
Brown dog, brown dog, sit on the floor

Write 8 periods on separate pieces of sentence strips. Set these aside.

If your child is a pre-reader, make simple drawings or find pictures in old catalogs or magazines of such items as a red truck, green frog, or yellow star. Glue these on separate pieces of sentence strips.

Picture Book about Colors

Choose a picture book about colors to read to your child. You may either pick an easy-reader scientific book that explains colors or a simple book listing different objects for various colors. *Make sure the text of the book has complete sentences.* When finished, go over several of the pages and ask your child to locate sentences that end with a period. Note that the next sentence always starts with a capital letter. If your child is interested, introduce other punctuation marks at this time such as question marks and exclamation points.

"Fun with Colors" Action Poem

1. Read the "Fun with Colors" action poem out loud. Ask your child to identify what is missing at the end of each sentence (a period).
2. Hand your child the pieces of sentence strips with the periods. Read over each sentence again, stopping after each one to give him an opportunity to place a period at the end.

3. Point out that each period is followed by a capital letter at the beginning of the next sentence.
4. Point out that titles do not end with periods.
5. After all the periods are added, read the poem again together, acting out each of the suggested movements.
6. When this activity is finished, remove all the periods and place them at the bottom of the sentence strips. Encourage your child to read the poem again later in the day, adding the periods at the end of the sentences and acting out the movements. If using a pocket chart, display this poem at the writing center throughout the following days of this lesson.

If your child does not yet know how to identify colors or read, write, and spell key words of this poem, use the sentence-strip pictures you made during Advanced Prep. Help him place each picture next to its corresponding words.

ACTIVITY SET 6:3

Guided Writing Practice

For the rest of Lesson 6, repeat the Guided Writing activity introduced in Activity Set 6:1. Write the following predictable sentence starters:

> **At a Glance: Activity Set 6:3**
>
> - Guided Writing Practice
> - Brainstorming

Today is
The season is
The weather is
Today is a ______ day because (insert a color word in the blank)
Today will be

Talk about ways to complete each of the sentences. Fill in the blank with a color word. If you made a *Portable Word Bank* of season words, pull it out to use again.

When the sentences are finished, ask her to help choose a title that includes her color word. Write the title at the top. Here is a sample of a completed Guided Writing Practice.

Yellow Daffodils
Today is Friday.
The season is spring.
The weather is windy and clear.
Today is a yellow day because the daffodils are blooming.
Today will be a day to pick yellow flowers.

Follow the same steps as in Guided Writing Practice, Activity Set 6:2.

1. Use the pointer yourself first as you read together.
2. Hand the pointer to your child and ask him to point to each word as you read the sentences together again. Guide his hand as needed.
3. Tell him to stop at the end of each sentence and point to the period.
4. Ask your child to put a sticker over each period.
5. Count the number of sentences and the number of periods. Compare these numbers with your child.
6. Ask him to locate the capital letter at the beginning of each sentence and place a star-shaped sticker above it.

Brainstorming - A Portable Word Bank of Color Words

Advance Prep

Use construction paper to cut out 1- x 2-inch rectangles for each color of the rainbow: red, orange, yellow, green, blue, and purple. Cut six of each color.

Directions

1. Sit down with your child and brainstorm a list of objects that are the colors of the rainbow. Write these words on paper. Suggestions include:
   - Red: *apple, fire truck, stop sign, strawberry, heart, cherry, ladybug, barn*
   - Orange: *fox, peach, butterfly, pumpkin, fire, basketball, carrot, clownfish*
   - Yellow: *sun, duck, chick, bus, lemon, sunflower, star, balloon, raincoat*
   - Green: *frog, grass, tree, pickle, alligator, celery, car, leaf, caterpillar, snake*
   - Blue: *sky, eyes, ocean, bird, marble, crayon, jeans, mailbox, blueberries*
   - Purple: *jelly, grapes, plum, crayon, grape juice, hat, paint, shirt, button*
2. Make a *Portable Word Bank* of vocabulary words your child can use to write her story. Here's how:
   - Have your child draw or glue a picture of a rainbow on the front of a manila file folder.
   - On the front of the file folder, write: *Words about Colors*
   - Help your child write one word on each appropriately-colored paper rectangle (from Advance Prep). Use the words from the brainstorming list as a guide. Example: Write *strawberry* on a red rectangle.
   - On the inside of the file folder, glue the paper rectangles to represent a rainbow of words.
3. On a separate piece of paper, make a simple graphic organizer to list ideas for the introduction, body, and closing of a story about one color. Label the graphic organizer as follows, leaving spaces for writing as you brainstorm together.

   Title:
Beginning:
Middle:
End:
4. Ask your child to choose one color for his story. Using the list of words for that color from the *Portable Word Bank*, ask him to think of story ideas. He may choose one word such as *alligator* to use as a main topic for his story. Or, if he is more advanced, he may choose several unrelated words from the word bank to create a silly story (*frog, gummy worm, leaf*).
5. As you discuss the ideas, talk about what might happen at the beginning of the story, in the middle, and at the end. Prompt a more reluctant child with questions. Discuss possible titles. Write these ideas down on your graphic organizer.

ACTIVITY SET 6:4

Guided Writing Practice

Write the following predictable sentence starters:

Today is
The season is
The weather is
Today is a ______ day because (insert a color word in the blank)
Today will be

At a Glance: Activity Set 6:4

- Guided Writing Practice
- The Writing Project
- Smaller Steps or Flying Higher

Talk about ways to complete each of the sentences. Fill in the blank with a color word. If you made a *Portable Word Bank* of season words, pull it out to use again.

When the sentences are finished, ask your child to help choose a title that includes his color word. Write the title at the top. Here is a sample of a completed Guided Writing Practice.

<u>Our Frosty White Day</u>
Today is Thursday.
The season is winter.
The weather is frosty and cold.
Today is a white day because we are making paper snowflakes.
Today will be a good day for hot chocolate!

Follow the same steps as in Guided Writing Practice, Activity Set 6:2. Here's how.

1. Use the pointer yourself first as you read together.
2. Hand the pointer to your child and ask him to point to each word as you read the sentences together again. Guide his hand as needed.
3. Tell your child to stop at the end of each sentence and point to the period.
4. Ask your child to put a sticker over each period.
5. Count the number of sentences and the number of periods. Compare these numbers with your child.
6. Ask him to locate the capital letter at the beginning of each sentence and place a star-shaped sticker above it.

The Writing Project - A Story about a Color

For the writing project, your child will write a story about one color. Her story will have at least five sentences with a beginning, a middle, and an end. (She may dictate to you or write independently as much as she can.) Write it on a piece of grade-level lined writing paper.

Here is a sample of a completed story.

Yellow Duck's Birthday
Today is yellow duck's birthday.
He got a yellow balloon.
He got a yellow hat.
He got a yellow ball.
Yellow duck had a happy birthday.

An older child might write a story like this.

Max's Brown Day
Max was a white dog.
He stayed clean and white inside the house.
One day he got out.
He dug a hole in the brown dirt.
He chewed the corner of the brown door mat.
Then he chased a brown truck down the street.
When he came back home, his owners were surprised.
Max was a brown dog!

Directions

Don't hesitate to prompt your child if she has trouble writing her story. Dialogue with her as you do during Guided Writing Practice, making sure you use her brainstorming ideas as a resource.

If she dictates the story to you:

1. Pause at the end of the first sentence, but do not write the period (or other punctuation mark). Ask her what comes at the end of the sentence. Write the period or appropriate punctuation mark.
2. Before you write the next sentence, ask what comes at the beginning of a new sentence (a capital letter). Write the next sentence, pausing again before you add the period.
3. Repeat this for each sentence you write from your child's dictation. When the story is finished, help her locate the period at the end of the first sentence of the story. Have her place a small round sticker over the period. Locate the capital letter at the beginning of the next sentence. Tell her to place a star-shaped sticker above it. Repeat this until she has found each period and each capital letter at the beginning of every sentence.

If your child writes the story independently:

1. Have her write on every other line of the paper. This leaves room to make corrections during the editing process.
2. Read through the finished story together and locate the first period. Have her place a small round sticker over the period. Locate the capital letter at the beginning of the next sentence. Tell her to place a star-shaped sticker above it. Repeat this until each period and each capital letter at the beginning of every sentence is found.

Smaller Steps - Encouraging Use of Repetitive Words

Encourage the use of repetitive words in the story of a younger learner. Repeating the same word over and over builds confidence in reading and writing skills.

Flying Higher - Writing a More Complex Story

An advanced or accelerated learner may enjoy using his word bank to write a more complex story about objects of many different colors.

ACTIVITY SET 6:5

Guided Writing Practice

Write the following predictable sentence starters:

> *Today is*
> *The season is*
> *The weather is*
> *Today is a ______ day because* (insert a color word in the blank)
> *Today will be*

At a Glance: Activity Set 6:5

- Guided Writing Practice
- Editing and Revising

Talk about ways to complete each of the sentences. Fill in the blank with a color word. If you made a *Portable Word Bank* of season words, pull it out to use again.

When the sentences are finished, ask your child to help choose a title that includes her color word. Write the title at the top.

After your Guided Writing Practice is written on paper, read it aloud two times as you have done on previous days. Use a pointer and stickers to identify periods and to locate the capital letter at the beginning of sentences.

Editing and Revising

Sit down with your child and her Writing Project story. Read the story together.

1. Discuss the structure of the story. Ask, "Does your story have a beginning, a middle, and an end?" "Does the title express the main idea?" If not, discuss ideas for improvement.
2. Examine each sentence with your child. Make sure each sentence has an end mark and begins with a capital letter.
3. Ask the child if each sentence makes a complete thought.
4. Use this time to help your child write down the changes to her story. Write the corrections on the paper itself or rewrite the corrected story on a new piece of paper.

ACTIVITY SET 6:6

Guided Writing Practice

Write the following predictable sentence starters:

Today is
The season is
The weather is
Today is a ______ day because (insert a color word in the blank)
Today will be

At a Glance: Activity Set 6:6

- Guided Writing Practice
- Activity Set Worksheet: "Colors in My World"

Talk about ways to complete each of the sentences. Fill in the blank with a color word. If you made a *Portable Word Bank* of season words, pull it out to use again.

When the sentences are finished, ask your child to help choose a title that includes his color word. Write the title at the top.

After your Guided Writing Practice is written on paper, read it aloud two times as you have done on previous days. Use a pointer and stickers to identify periods and to locate the capital letter at the beginning of sentences.

Activity Set Worksheet: "Colors in My World"

Use Lesson 6: "Colors in My World" Activity Set Worksheet.

1. Have your child cut out the periods along the bottom of the page and glue them where they belong.
2. Have him color the pictures the corresponding color.
3. On the back of the page, tell him to draw an object of any color he chooses. Encourage him to write at least one sentence about his picture, putting a capital letter at the beginning and a period at the end.

ACTIVITY SET 6:7

Guided Writing Practice

Write the following predictable sentence starters:

> *Today is*
> *The season is*
> *The weather is*
> *Today is a ______ day because* (insert a color word in the blank)
> *Today will be*

At a Glance: Activity Set 6:7

- Guided Writing Practice
- Publishing the Project

Talk about ways to complete each of the sentences. Fill in the blank with a color word. If you made a *Portable Word Bank* of season words, pull it out to use again.

When the sentences are finished, ask your child to help choose a title that includes his color word. Write the title at the top.

After your Guided Writing Practice is written on paper, read it aloud two times as you have done on previous days. Use a pointer and stickers to identify periods and to locate the capital letter at the beginning of sentences.

Publishing the Project - Making a Story Pocket

Advance Prep

Cut a paper plate in half. Place both pieces face to face and staple together around the curved edges. The top straight edges remain open to form a pocket.

Publish your child's Writing Project story in a "pocket" for him to share with others. Here's how.

1. Allow time for him to use crayons, markers, or paint to decorate the paper plate pocket so it matches the color of the story.
2. Glue the story to the front of the paper plate pocket or fold the paper and store it inside the pocket.
3. Have your child draw a picture of each object in his story on cardboard, poster board, or tag board.
4. Cut out the tag board pieces and store them in the pocket.
5. Encourage your child to read his story to family members or a friend, pulling out the corresponding pieces from the pocket and placing them on the table as he shares.

ACTIVITY SET 6:8

Guided Writing Practice

Write the following predictable sentence starters:

Today is
The season is
The weather is
Today is a ______ day because (insert a color word in the blank)
Today will be

At a Glance: Activity Set 6:8

- Guided Writing Practice
- Evaluating the Student's Work
- Want to Do More? (optional) Writing Across the Curriculum: Spotlight on Visual Arts

Talk about ways to complete each of the sentences. Fill in the blank with a color word. If you made a *Portable Word Bank* of season words, pull it out to use again.

When the sentences are finished, ask her to help choose a title that includes her color word. Write the title at the top.

After your Guided Writing Practice is written on paper, read it aloud two times as you have done on previous days. Use a pointer and stickers to identify periods and to locate the capital letter at the beginning of sentences.

Evaluating the Student's Work

Evaluate your student's work using the Primary Writing Skills Evaluation Chart for Lessons 6-10 found in the Activity Set Worksheet Pack. Remove it and keep it in a folder or file.

Want to Do More?

Writing Across the Curriculum: Spotlight on Visual Arts in Famous Paintings
Look at paintings done by famous artists. Read an art book together, look at famous paintings on the Internet, or take a field trip to an art museum. Discuss the artist's use of color. Here's how:

1. Choose a favorite picture.
2. Ask your child to describe the colors in that picture. Have him write down at least one sentence each for several of the colors the artist used in the painting, explaining how each color is used in the picture. For example, "The man's shirt is yellow" or "I like that pink flower," or "Why did they paint the sky green?" (Your child may dictate these sentences to you or write independently as much as he can.)
3. When finished writing, have your child place a small round sticker over each period and put a star-shaped sticker above the capital letter at the beginning of each sentence.

Lesson 7:
Writing with Rhyme

Lesson Focus: Using Word Families to Write Stories with Rhyming Words
Theme: Rhymes

Objectives

Your child will:

- Review the use of punctuation in a sentence.
- Learn to identify various word families.
- Become familiar with words that rhyme.
- Use rhyming words to write a story.

Materials

Guided Writing Practice

- Pointers
- Tablet or chart paper and markers
- Small round stickers (1/4- or 1/2-inch)
- Star-shaped stickers

Pre-writing Activities

- Picture book written in verse or a book of children's poems
- Construction or scrapbooking paper in a variety of solid colors, including green
- White computer or copy paper
- Scissors, hole punch, markers, glue
- Three-ring binder

Brainstorming

- Tablet or chart paper and markers

The Writing Project

- Grade-level writing paper
- Pencils or markers

Activity Set Worksheet

- Pencils, crayons, or markers

Publishing the Project

- Computer or copy paper
- Pencils, crayons, or markers

Want to Do More?

- Writing Across the Curriculum
  - ~ Paper dinner plate divided into three sections
  - ~ Paper bowls
  - ~ Small paper cup
  - ~ Plastic knife, fork, and spoon
  - ~ 12- x 18-inch construction paper
  - ~ Construction or scrapbooking paper in a variety of colors including green, brown, and white
  - ~ Scissors, markers, glue
- Computer Capers
  - ~ Card-making program

ACTIVITY SET 7:1

Guided Writing Practice

At a Glance: Activity Set 7:1

- Guided Writing Practice

Sit side-by-side with your child and write on a tablet, or use an easel with chart paper. Spend no more than 5-10 minutes on this activity. Use a marker and write the following predictable sentence starters:

Good morning
Today is
It is
We will
Today will be

Discuss various options for ideas on how to complete each of the five sentences. When the sentences are finished, ask your child to help choose a title. Write the title at the top. Here's an idea of how to get started with today's Guided Writing Practice.

You:	*Let's say "good morning" to someone. Whom should we pick?*
Child:	Me!
You:	*All right. Good morning to you! Let's write that down. Good morning to you. Pick a marker and help me write some of these words.*
You:	*Now let's look at the calendar. What day is today?*
Child:	Monday.
You:	*Today is Monday. Say it as a complete thought. "Today is Monday."*
Child:	Today is Monday.
You:	*Great. Let's write that on our paper. Can you help?*

Here is a sample of a completed Guided Writing Practice.

A Happy Hamster Day
Good morning to you.
Today is Monday.
It is time to clean the hamster cage.
We will make Hamlet happy.
Today will be Hamlet's happy day.

Help your child identify periods and capital letters. Here's how.

1. Using a pointer yourself, read over the sentences together. At the end of each sentence, point to the period and pause before going on.

2. When you have finished, ask your child to locate the periods and place a small round sticker over each one. Have her place a star-shaped sticker above the capital letters at the beginning of each sentence.
3. Ask your child to choose a pointer to point to each word as you once more read the sentences together.
4. This time, use the pointer yourself to read over the sentences again. Read the sentences slowly to give time for your child to respond. Instruct your child to:
    - Stand up each time you reach a capital letter at the beginning of the sentence.
    - Hop when you reach a capital letter in the middle of a sentence.
    - Sit down when you reach a period.

You will use the same predictable sentence starters every day of Lesson 7.

ACTIVITY SET 7:2

Guided Writing Practice

Write the following predictable sentence starters:

Good morning
Today is
It is
We will
Today will be

At a Glance: Activity Set 7:2

- Guided Writing Practice
- Pre-writing Activities: Picture book with text that rhymes

Discuss various options for ideas on how to complete each of the five sentences. Encourage your child to write as many letters or words as she can. When the sentences are finished, ask her to help choose a title. Write the title at the top. Here is a sample of a completed Guided Writing Practice.

<u>It Is Too Hot</u>
Good morning, everyone!
Today is Wednesday.
It is so, so hot today.
We will not be able to play outside.
Today will be a good day for some cold lemonade.

Continue to help your child identify periods and capital letters.

1. Using a pointer yourself, read over the sentences together. At the end of each sentence, point to the period and pause before going on.
2. When you have finished, ask your child to locate the period and place a small round sticker over each one. Have her place a star-shaped sticker above the capital letters at the beginning of each sentence.
3. Ask your child to choose a pointer to point to each word as you once more read the sentences together.
4. Use the pointer yourself to read over the sentences again. Read the sentences slowly to give time for your child to respond. Instruct your child to:
   - stand up each time you reach a capital letter at the beginning of the sentence;
   - hop when you reach a capital letter in the middle of a sentence; and
   - sit down when you reach a period.

Pre-writing Activities

Advance Prep

1. Glue a green paper stem and two leaves to a sheet of white copy paper.
2. Glue a 3-inch circle flower center at the top of the stem. Make five of these, one for each vowel of the alphabet.
3. Write one word family or ending rhyme on each flower center. Use simpler word families with younger children, such as:

   -at for the vowel *a*

   -en for the vowel *e*

   -op for the vowel *o*
4. With older or more advanced students, also include endings like:

   -ing for the vowel *i*

   -ump for the vowel *u*

   -ake for the vowel *a*
5. Cut out at least 25 flower petals from construction or scrapbooking paper. They can be different colors but should all be the same size.

Picture Book with Text That Rhymes

Choose a picture book to read to your child that is written in rhyme, or read several rhyming poems from a children's collection of poetry. When finished, go over several of the pages and find pairs of rhyming words.

Word Family Flowers

Introduce your child to word families by making *word family flowers*. Here's how.

1. Together with your child, write rhyming words from each word family on the flower petals, one word per petal. Write words such as:

   -at: *bat, cat, fat, hat, mat, pat, rat, sat, vat*

   -en: *Ben, den, hen, Jen, Ken, Len, men, pen, ten, when*

   -op: *cop, flop, hop, mop, pop, stop, top*

   -ing: *fling, king, ring, sing, spring, string, swing, thing, wing*

   -ump: *bump, clump, dump, hump, jump, lump, pump, stump*

   -ake: *bake, cake, lake, make, quake, rake, shake, snake, take, wake*

2. Glue the petals around the center of the corresponding flowers.
3. When finished making the *word family flowers*, punch holes in each page and place in a three-ring binder. Label the binder *My Garden of Rhyming Words*.

Alternate Idea: Draw Your Flowers

1. With a marker, draw a 3-inch circle on a large scrap of construction paper. Make five of these, one for each vowel of the alphabet. Write one word family or ending rhyme in the center of each flower. For example:

   -an for the vowel *a*

   -et for the vowel *e*

   -ig for the vowel *i*

   -ock for the vowel *o*

   -unk for the vowel *u*

2. Draw 6-10 petals surrounding each flower's center. Together with your child, write rhyming words from that word family in the petals, one word per petal. Write words such as:

   -an: *an, can, Dan, fan, Jan, man, pan, ran, tan, van*

   -et: *bet, get, jet, let, met, net, pet, set, vet, wet*

   -ig: *big, dig, fig, jig, pig, twig, wig*

   -ock: *clock, dock, flock, lock, knock, peacock, rock, sock*

   -unk: *bunk, dunk, gunk, hunk, junk, skunk, stunk, trunk*

3. Draw a stem on five sheets of white copy paper. Cut out each flower and glue it onto the stem. Add drawn or cut-out leaves to complete each word family flower.
4. When finished, punch holes in each page and place in a three-ring binder. Label the binder *My Garden of Rhyming Words.*

Over upcoming lessons, continue to make more *word family flowers* or add new words to these flowers until your notebook contains more pages. This notebook will provide a handy reference during Lesson 4 of Book B when you teach your child to write a poem or nursery rhyme.

ACTIVITY SET 7:3

Guided Writing Practice

Write the following predictable sentence starters:

> *Good morning*
> *Today is*
> *It is*
> *We will*
> *Today will be*

At a Glance: Activity Set 7:3

- Guided Writing Practice
- Brainstorming

Discuss various options for ideas on how to complete each of the five sentences. Encourage your child to write as many letters or words as he can.

Beginning today, reinforce the concept of rhyming words to your child during Guided Writing Practice by encouraging him to use two or more rhyming words. Your child's *word family flowers* may help. He can use two rhyming words in the same sentence or he can create a rhyme using two sentences. Here are some ideas.

> Today is *Monday*. It is a *fun day.*
> It is *snowing* and *blowing* outside.
> It is time to ride *bikes* and *trikes.*
> We will throw the *ball* in the *hall.*
> We will eat a *sweet treat.*
> We will do dog tricks with *Spot*. Today will be *hot.*
> Today will be a *silly, nilly, willy*, day.

Here's an idea for helping your child use words that rhyme.

You: *Last time we learned about rhyming words, and we made word family flowers. Today we're going to use some rhyming words during writing time. Can you think of some words that rhyme?*

Child: Ball, fall.

You: *Fantastic! Now look at our paper. So far, we have:*

> *Good morning, Matthew.*
>
> *Today is Friday.*
>
> *Next, it says: "It is _____." Tell me about today. It is. . .what?*

Child: It is … I don't know.

You: *Shall we write something about our day? What are we doing today?*

Child: After lunch we get to go to the library.

You: *So you can say: It is _____.*

Child: It is our library day?

You: Good! Let's write that. It is our library day. And what do we do at the library?

Child: You let us read one book, and then we get to bring some home.

You: Did you say book? What rhymes with book?

Child: Cook. Shook. Look. Took.

You: You're so smart! Let's try to use rhyming words in our next sentence: "We will ____." We will. . .what?

Child: Read a book.

You: Yes, but let's think of a word that rhymes with book.

Child: Look?

You: That's perfect! Now, can you turn that into a complete sentence using look *and* book*? "We will ____."*

Child: We will look at a book.

You: Wow! Look, book. *You made a rhyme!*

Continue prompting your child. When the sentences are finished, ask him to help choose a title. Write the title at the top. Here are two samples that use rhyming words.

Going to the Library
Good morning, Matthew.
Today is Thursday.
It is our library day.
We will *look* at a *book*.
Today will be a good day for some horse books.

Blocks and Rocks
Good morning, Angelo!
Today is Friday.
It is a good day to play with *blocks* and *rocks*.
We will make a tall castle and a fort.
Today will be a building day.

Continue to help your child identify periods and capital letters.

1. Using a pointer yourself, read over the sentences together. At the end of each sentence, point to the period and pause before going on.
2. When you have finished, ask your child to locate the period and place a small round sticker over each one. Have him place a star-shaped sticker above the capital letters at the beginning of each sentence.

3. Ask your child to choose a pointer to point to each word as you once more read the sentences together.
4. Use the pointer yourself to read over the sentences again. Read the sentences slowly to give time for your child to respond. Instruct your child to:
   - Stand up each time you reach a capital letter at the beginning of the sentence.
   - Hop when you reach a capital letter in the middle of a sentence.
   - Sit down when you reach a period.

Brainstorming - Making a Graphic Organizer

Directions

1. Brainstorm a list of 5-10 word families and corresponding words. Write these words on paper. Suggestions include:

   -ack: *back, Jack, Mack, pack, quack, rack, sack, stack, tack, Zack*
   -ail: *bail, Gail, jail, mail, nail, pail, quail, rail, sail, snail, tail*
   -an: *an, can, Dan, fan, man, Nan, pan, ran, Stan, tan, van*
   -ark: *bark, Clark, dark, lark, Mark, park, shark*
   -eep: *beep, cheep, deep, jeep, keep, peep, sheep, sleep, weep*
   -ell: *bell, fell, jell, sell, shell, spell, tell, well*
   -et: *bet, get, jet, let, met, net, pet, set, vet, wet*
   -ice: *dice, ice, lice, mice, nice, rice, slice, twice*
   -ick: *brick, chick, click, flick, lick, Nick, pick, Rick, sick, stick, trick*
   -ig: *big, dig, fig, jig, pig, twig, wig*
   -ock: *clock, dock, flock, lock, knock, peacock, rock, sock*
   -og: *bog, dog, fog, frog, hog, jog, log*
   -ug: *bug, dug, hug, jug, mug, pug, rug, tug*
   -un: *bun, fun, nun, pun, run, sun*
   -ub: *club, cub, grub, rub, sub, tub*
   -unk: *bunk, dunk, gunk, hunk, junk, skunk, stunk, trunk*

   Other common word families include: *-ain, -ake, -ale, -all, -ame, -ank, -ap, -ash, -at, -ate, -aw -ay, -eat, -est, -ide, -ight, -ill, -in, -ine, -ink, -ip, -it, -oke, -op, -ore, -ot.*

2. On a separate piece of paper, make a simple graphic organizer to list ideas for the introduction, body, and closing of a story using words that rhyme. It should look something like this:

   Title:
   Beginning:
   Middle:
   End:

3. From one or more word families, ask your child to choose rhyming words he'd like to use in a story. As you discuss his ideas, talk about what might happen at the beginning of the story, in the middle, and at the end. Discuss possible titles.
4. Write these ideas down on your graphic organizer.

ACTIVITY SET 7:4

Guided Writing Practice

For the rest of Lesson 7, repeat the Guided Writing activity introduced in Activity Set 7:3. Write the following predictable sentence starters:

> *Good morning*
> *Today is*
> *It is*
> *We will*
> *Today will be*

At a Glance: Activity Set 7:4

- Guided Writing Practice
- The Writing Project
- Smaller Steps or Flying Higher

Your child will continue to complete each of the five sentences and will use *two or more rhyming words* in her Guided Writing story. Encourage your child to write as many letters or words as she can.

When the sentences are finished, ask her to help choose a title. Write the title at the top. Here is a sample of a completed Guided Writing Practice.

> <u>Baking with Nana</u>
> Good morning, Nana!
> Today is Tuesday.
> It is a special day because Nana came to our house.
> We will *bake* a *cake* for dessert.
> Today will be a delicious chocolate cake day!

Continue to help your child identify periods and capital letters.

1. Using a pointer yourself, read over the sentences together. At the end of each sentence, point to the period and pause before going on.
2. When you have finished, ask your child to locate the period and place a small round sticker over each one. Have her place a star-shaped sticker above the capital letters at the beginning of each sentence.
3. Ask your child to choose a pointer to point to each word as you once more read the sentences together.
4. Use the pointer yourself to read over the sentences again. Read the sentences slowly to give time for your child to respond. Instruct her to:
   - Stand up each time you reach a capital letter at the beginning of the sentence.
   - Hop when you reach a capital letter in the middle of a sentence.
   - Sit down when you reach a period.

The Writing Project - A Story Using Rhyming Words

For the writing project, your child will write a story using rhyming words from one or more word families.

Directions

1. Her story will have a beginning, a middle, and an end.
2. The story will contain five or more sentences.
3. Your child may dictate to you or write independently as much as she can. Write the story on a piece of grade-level writing paper, skipping every other line to allow room for editing and revising.
4. Here is a sample of a completed story.

    The Bird That Liked to Sing
    There once was a bird that liked to sing.
    The bird had a pretty blue ring.
    It liked to wear the ring on its wing.
    It liked to sing when it was wearing the ring.
    I liked to listen to the bird sing.

Smaller Steps - Vocabulary: Making More Paper Coins

The vocabulary of a younger learner can build quickly as she works with rhyming words from the same word families. If she hasn't already made one, follow the instructions in Activity Set 5:8 to make a paper wallet or purse and gold coins. Have her write each new word she's learned during this lesson on a paper gold coin and add it to her collection.

Flying Higher - Writing a Poem

Challenge an accelerated or advanced student to use words that rhyme at the end of each sentence and write a poem.

ACTIVITY SET 7:5

Guided Writing Practice

Write the following predictable sentence starters:

> *Good morning*
> *Today is*
> *It is*
> *We will*
> *Today will be*

At a Glance: Activity Set 7:5

- Guided Writing Practice
- Editing and Revising

Your child will continue to complete each of the five sentences and will use *two or more rhyming words* in her Guided Writing story.

When the sentences are finished, ask her to help choose a title. Write the title at the top.

After your Guided Writing Practice is written on paper, read it aloud two times as you have done on previous days. Use the pointer and stickers to identify periods and capital letters.

Using the pointer yourself, read over the sentences once more. Instruct your child to:

- Stand up each time you reach a capital letter at the beginning of the sentence.
- Hop when you reach a capital letter in the middle of a sentence.
- Sit down when you reach a period.

Editing and Revising

Sit down with your child and his Writing Project story. Read the story together.

1. Ask him to point out the rhyming words and identify the word family it belongs to.
2. Discuss the structure of the story. Ask, "Does your story have a beginning, a middle, and an end?" "Does the title express the main idea?" If not, discuss ideas for improvement.
3. Ask the child if each sentence makes a complete thought.
4. Examine each sentence with your child. Make sure each sentence has an end mark and begins with a capital letter.
5. Use this time to help him write down the changes to his story. Write the corrections on the paper itself.

ACTIVITY SET 7:6

Guided Writing Practice

Write the following predictable sentence starters:

> *Good morning*
> *Today is*
> *It is*
> *We will*
> *Today will be*

At a Glance: Activity Set 7:6

- Guided Writing Practice
- Activity Set Worksheet: "Rhyme Time"

Your child will continue to complete each of the five sentences and will use *two or more rhyming words* in her Guided Writing story.

When the sentences are finished, ask her to help choose a title. Write the title at the top.

After your Guided Writing Practice is written on paper, read it aloud two times as you have done on previous days. Use the pointer and stickers to identify periods and capital letters.

Using the pointer yourself, read over the sentences once more. Instruct your child to:

- Stand up each time you reach a capital letter at the beginning of the sentence.
- Hop when you reach a capital letter in the middle of a sentence.
- Sit down when you reach a period.

Activity Set Worksheet: "Rhyme Time"

Use Lesson 7: "Rhyme Time" Activity Set Worksheet.

Lesson 7

Rhyme Time

Name: ____________________

Look at the pictures and write the words that rhyme.

What a silly ________.

It likes to wear a **cape**.

Just look at **Ned**.

He is jumping on the ________.

Get away from the ________.

It is going to **tip**.

I hear tick-**tock**.

It is a very loud ________.

Do not go near the tree **trunk**.

I smell a ________.

Your turn. Write a sentence with these words that rhyme.

bug

rug

1. Read over the sentences with your child. Identify each of the rebus pictures. Have her write the words on the lines.
2. Have your child write a sentence using the words *bug* and *rug*.
3. On the back of the page, your child can draw a picture and practice writing pairs of rhyming words (*cake, rake; hat, bat*). Or, she can write sentences that contain several rhyming words (For *lunch* I will *munch* on a *bunch* of grapes). For inspiration, let her browse through the *word family flowers* in her *Garden of Rhyming Words* notebook.

ACTIVITY SET 7:7

Guided Writing Practice

Write the following predictable sentence starters:

> *Good morning*
> *Today is*
> *It is*
> *We will*
> *Today will be*

At a Glance: Activity Set 7:7

- Guided Writing Practice
- Publishing the Project

Your child will continue to complete each of the five sentences and will use *two or more rhyming words* in her Guided Writing story.

When the sentences are finished, ask her to help choose a title. Write the title at the top.

After your Guided Writing Practice is written on paper, read it aloud two times as you have done on previous days. Use the pointer and stickers to identify periods and capital letters.

Using the pointer yourself, read over the sentences once more. Instruct your child to:

- Stand up each time you reach a capital letter at the beginning of the sentence.
- Hop when you reach a capital letter in the middle of a sentence.
- Sit down when you reach a period.

Publishing the Project - Making a Rebus

Transform your child's story into a rebus. Here's how.

1. Together with your child (according to his ability), type the story on a computer. Leave a large blank space next to each rhyming word that will be easy for your child to illustrate. If you don't have a computer, simply write out the story neatly by hand, leaving a large blank space next to as many rhyming words as possible.
2. Encourage your child to draw a picture in each space to illustrate the key rhyming words.
3. Not all words need to be illustrated. For one thing, sometimes there's no way to illustrate a particular word, such as *let*, *keep*, or *tell*. Additionally, some children don't have the patience to do a lot of drawing. If your child easily tires of drawing, consider taking turns creating pictures for the rebus.
4. Read the rebus with a friend or family member.

Example based on Writing Project:

<u>The Bird That Liked to Sing</u>

There once was a bird that liked to sing  .

The bird had a pretty blue ring  .

It liked to wear the ring  on its wing  .

It liked to sing  when it was wearing the ring  .

I liked to listen to the bird sing .

ACTIVITY SET 7:8

Guided Writing Practice

Write the following predictable sentence starters:

> *Good morning*
> *Today is*
> *It is*
> *We will*
> *Today will be*

Your child will continue to complete each of the five sentences and will use *two or more rhyming words* in her Guided Writing story.

When the sentences are finished, ask her to help choose a title. Write the title at the top.

At a Glance: Activity Set 7:8

- Guided Writing Practice
- Evaluating the Student's Work
- Want to Do More? (optional) Writing Across the Curriculum: Spotlight on Health and Nutrition
- Want to Do More? (optional) Computer Capers

After your Guided Writing Practice is written on paper, read it aloud two times as you have done on previous days. Use the pointer and stickers to identify periods and capital letters.

Using the pointer yourself, read over the sentences once more. Instruct your child to:

- Stand up each time you reach a capital letter at the beginning of the sentence.
- Hop when you reach a capital letter in the middle of a sentence.
- Sit down when you reach a period.

Evaluating the Student's Work

Use the Primary Writing Skills Evaluation Chart for Lessons 6-10 to evaluate your student's work.

Want to Do More?

Writing Across the Curriculum: Spotlight on Health and Nutrition - Making a "Rhyming Foods" Placemat

Advance Prep

- Make ten brown paper circles to resemble meatballs. Write five pairs of rhyming words from various word families, one word on each meatball. Place the meatballs in a paper bowl.
- Make ten white paper ovals to resemble potatoes. Write five pairs of rhyming words from various word families, one word on each potato. Place the potatoes in their own paper bowl.
- Make ten green paper rectangles to resemble green beans. Write five pairs of rhyming words from various word families, one word on each green bean. Place the green beans in their own paper bowl.
- Make ten shapes of different colors of paper to resemble pieces of fruit in a fruit salad. Write five pairs of rhyming words from various word families, one word on each piece of fruit. Place the fruit in its own paper bowl.

Make a Rhyming Foods Placemat with your child. Here's how.

1. Glue a dinner-sized paper plate divided into three sections, a paper bowl, a small paper cup, and plastic silverware onto a large piece of 12- x 18-inch construction paper to resemble a place setting.
2. Place the serving bowls of food next to your child's placemat. Discuss a healthy balance of nutrition complete with protein, vegetables, fruits, and grains. Use this time to introduce the food pyramid.
3. Encourage your child to dish up a healthy serving of each food group by finding two words from the same word family in each serving bowl. Place the two rhyming meatballs, two rhyming potatoes, and two rhyming green beans on the plate. Place the two rhyming pieces of fruit in the bowl.
4. Have your child write a story using the pairs of rhyming words she chose.

Computer Capers - Making a Restaurant Menu

Make a restaurant menu of word families. Here's how.

1. Use the half-fold card feature on a card-making program. Design the front with pictures of food and of people dining.
2. On the inside left of the menu (page 2 of the card program), include topics such as snacks, main dishes, and desserts.
3. Under each topic, insert clip art pictures of an assortment of food. Choose food items with simple names and rhymes, such as: *ham, fish, bean, meat, nut, chip, pear, peach, grape, plum, cake, pie, bun*, and *drink*.

4. Next to the picture of each food item, type words in the same word family. Here is a sample menu page:

Janie's Famous Restaurant

Menu

Snacks

–ip: chip, clip, dip, flip, hip, lip, rip, sip, ship, snip, tip, zip

–ear: pear, bear, tear, wear

–ut: nut, but, cut, gut, hut, jut, rut

Main Dishes

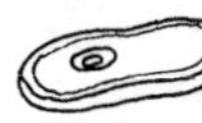
–am: ham, clam, dam, jam, Pam, ram, Sam, yam

–eat: meat, beat, cleat, heat, neat, seat

–ish: fish, dish, swish, wish

Desserts

–ake: cake, bake, Jake, lake, make, rake, shake, take, wake

–ie: pie, die, lie, tie

–un: bun, fun, nun, pun, run, spun, sun

5. On the inside right of the menu (page 3 of the card program), type an original story using words selected from the word families on page 114. *If your child does not want to write a new story, type in the story he wrote for either the writing project or the optional Writing Across the Curriculum project.*
6. Decorate the back of the menu with a picture or a description about the author—your child!
7. Print out the menu and fold it in half according to the card program's directions.
8. Play restaurant with your child. When it's time to order your meal, choose one food from each section of the menu. Say the corresponding word family and read its list of rhyming words.
9. For fun, serve up a real snack! As you munch, read the story together.

Lesson 8: Organizing Ideas

Lesson Focus: Using A Story Web to Organize Ideas
Theme: Insects and Bugs

Objectives

Your child will:

- Practice observing items she plans to write about.
- Organize facts and information on a story web.
- Learn to refer to a story web as she writes.
- Write a simple nonfiction article.
- Practice writing independently as much as possible.

Materials

Guided Writing Practice

- Pointers
- Tablet or chart paper and markers

Pre-writing Activities

- *My Garden of Rhyming Words* notebook from Activity Set 7:2
  - ~ Construction or scrapbooking paper in a variety of solid colors, including green
  - ~ White computer or copy paper
  - ~ Scissors, hole punch, markers, glue
- Nonfiction picture book about insects or spiders
- Notepad and pencil
- Cardboard milk carton
- Old sheer nylon stocking
- Scissors
- Optional butterfly net and magnifying glass

Brainstorming

- Tablet or chart paper and markers

The Writing Project

- Grade-level writing paper
- Pencils or markers

Activity Set Worksheet

- Pencils, crayons, or markers
- *Story Idea Box* from Activity Set 3:3

Publishing the Project

- Computer or copy paper
- Lightweight 10-inch paper plates
- Yarn
- Scissors, hole punch
- Pencils, markers, crayons
- Clear tape or glue

Want to Do More?

- Writing Across the Curriculum
    - ~ Tablet or chart paper with markers
    - ~ Large sheets of butcher paper in a light color
    - ~ Tissue paper or shredded newspaper
    - ~ Pencils, markers, or crayons
    - ~ Scissors, stapler

ACTIVITY SET 8:1

Guided Writing Practice

Sit side-by-side with your child and write on a tablet. Or, use an easel with chart paper. Use a marker and write the following predictable sentence starters:

Hello
Today is
It is
We will
I think

> **At a Glance: Activity Set 8:1**
> - Guided Writing Practice
> - Pre-writing Activity (optional)

Discuss various options for ideas on how to complete each of the five sentences. Encourage your child to write as many letters or words as he can. When the sentences are finished, ask your child to help choose a title. Write the title at the top. Here is a sample of a completed Guided Writing Practice.

Music Day
Hello, Bryce.
Today is Monday.
It is 10:00 in the morning.
We will listen to music today.
I think we will sing and dance.

Help your child identify periods and capital letters, following the same steps as in Lesson 7. Here's how.

1. Using a pointer yourself, read over the sentences together. At the end of each sentence, point to the period and pause before going on.
2. Ask your child to choose a pointer to point to each word as you once more read the sentences together.
3. Use the pointer yourself to read over the sentences again. Read the sentences slowly to give time for your child to respond. Instruct your child to:
   - stand up each time you reach a capital letter at the beginning of the sentence;
   - hop when you reach a capital letter in the middle of a sentence; and
   - sit down when you reach a period.

You will use the same predictable sentence starters every day of Lesson 8.

Pre-writing Activity (optional) - Word Family Flowers

If time permits sometime during Lesson 8, make another word family flower or add new words to existing flowers in your *Garden of Rhyming Words* notebook. This notebook will provide a handy reference in Lesson 4 of Book B when you teach your child to write a poem or nursery rhyme. You will also find this notebook handy any time your child writes with rhyme.

If your child has not yet made a *Garden of Rhyming Words* notebook, see Activity Set 7:2 for instructions and a list of word families.

ACTIVITY SET 8:2

Guided Writing Practice

At a Glance: Activity Set 8:2

- Guided Writing Practice
- Pre-writing Activities: Picture book about insects or spiders

Write the following predictable sentence starters:

Hello
Today is
It is
We will
I think

Discuss various options for ideas on how to complete each of the five sentences. Encourage your child to write as many letters or words as he can. When the sentences are finished, ask your child to help choose a title. Write the title at the top. Here is a sample of a completed Guided Writing Practice.

A Rainy Tuesday
Hello, School Room!
Today is Tuesday.
It is raining outside.
We will stay in the house and do our schoolwork.
I think it will be sunny tomorrow.

Continue to help your child identify periods and capital letters.

1. Using a pointer yourself, read over the sentences together. At the end of each sentence, point to the period and pause before going on.
2. Ask your child to choose a pointer to point to each word as you once more read the sentences together.
3. Use the pointer yourself to read over the sentences again. Read the sentences slowly to give time for your child to respond. Instruct your child to:
   - Stand up each time you reach a capital letter at the beginning of the sentence.
   - Hop when you reach a capital letter in the middle of a sentence.
   - Sit down when you reach a period.

Pre-writing Activities

Advance Prep

Make an insect house by cutting out several windows on a cardboard milk carton. Cover the carton with an old, sheer nylon stocking.

Picture Book about Insects or Spiders

Choose a nonfiction picture book about insects or spiders to read to your child.

Take a Bug Walk

Take a nature walk together to observe bugs and insects.

1. Provide a small notepad for your child. For extra fun, bring along a butterfly net or magnifying glass.
2. When you find a bug on your walk, place it inside the milk carton. Cover the carton with the stocking while you observe the insect inside.
3. Look at the bug with your child. Encourage him to draw a picture of it on the notepad or write down at least five observations such as: six legs, red and black, or as big as my thumbnail. Release the bug when your observation is finished and look for another.
4. If weather prohibits a walk, look at insects in a book, encyclopedia, or on the Internet. Use the notepad to sketch pictures of favorite bugs and write down interesting observations.

ACTIVITY SET 8:3

Guided Writing Practice

Write the following predictable sentence starters:

> *Hello*
> *Today is*
> *It is*
> *We will*
> *I think*

At a Glance: Activity Set 8:3

- Guided Writing Practice
- Brainstorming

Talk about ways to complete each sentence. Encourage your child to write as many letters or words as she can. When finished, ask her to help choose a title. Write the title at the top. Here is an example.

> Making a Map
> Hello, Jillian.
> Today is Wednesday.
> It is our day to make a map.
> We will make a map of Egypt.
> I think I will put it in my notebook.

After your Guided Writing Practice is written on paper, read it aloud two times as you have done on previous days. Use the pointer and stickers to identify periods and capital letters. Using the pointer yourself, read over the sentences once more. Instruct your child to:

- Stand up each time you reach a capital letter at the beginning of the sentence.
- Hop when you reach a capital letter in the middle of a sentence.
- Sit down when you reach a period.

Brainstorming - Making a Story Web

1. Draw a simple story web on paper with a circle in the middle and five or six lines extending out from the circle to resemble a spider's web.
2. In the center of the circle, write the topic: Bugs.
3. On each of the lines, list the information that supports the topic. Use the notepad of observations as a source.

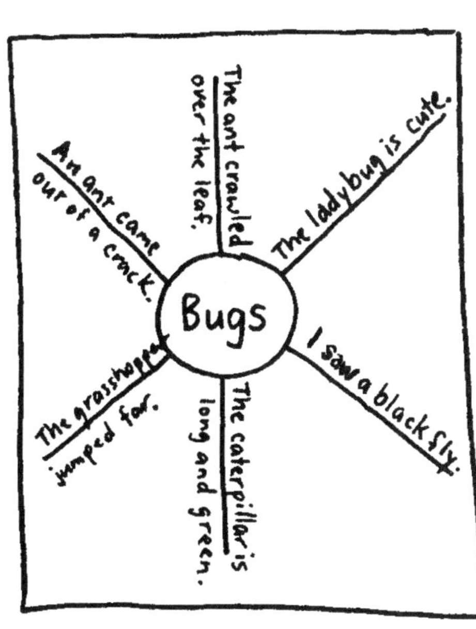

4. For a younger learner, write one word on each line of the story web listing the names of the insects she observed, such as:
   - *beetle*
   - *ant*
   - *fly*
   - *bee*
   - *ladybug*
   - *aphid*
5. For an accelerated or more verbal student, write one sentence on each line of the story web, such as:
   - *The black beetle ran away.*
   - *The ant walked into a hole.*
   - *The fly went by my head.*
   - *The bee was looking for a flower.*
   - *The ladybug was pretty.*
   - *I saw an aphid on a pink rose.*

Each sentence can be about *any* bug the child saw on her walk.

Directions

1. On a separate piece of paper, make a simple graphic organizer like the one in Activity Set 5:3 to list ideas for the beginning, middle, and ending of your child's upcoming writing project about bugs. Your child will write a nonfiction article for this lesson rather than create a make-believe (fictional) story as before. Therefore, label the graphic organizer as follows, leaving spaces for writing as you brainstorm together:

   Title:
   Introduction:
   Body:
   Closing:
2. Discuss potential introductions such as:
   - *Today we took a bug walk.*
   - *Bugs come in all shapes and sizes.*
   - *I found some bugs in my yard.*
3. Look at the story web with your child to choose three or more nuggets of supporting information to include in the body of the article. Write these on the graphic organizer.

4. Ask your child how he would like to end his article. Talk about possible closings such as:
   - *I set the bugs free again and came home.*
   - *My favorite one of all was the yellow spider.*
   - *I want to look for more bugs again tomorrow.*
5. Brainstorm possible titles and write these on the graphic organizer.

ACTIVITY SET 8:4

Guided Writing Practice

Write the following predictable sentence starters:

Hello
Today is
It is
We will
I think

At a Glance: Activity Set 8:4

- Guided Writing Practice
- The Writing Project
- Smaller Steps or Flying Higher

Talk about ways to complete each sentence. Encourage your child to write as many letters or words as she can. When finished, ask her to help choose a title. Write the title at the top. Here is an example.

<u>Lunchtime</u>
Hello, William.
Today is Friday.
It is almost lunchtime.
We will have peanut butter sandwiches.
I think I will choose grape jelly.

After your Guided Writing Practice is written on paper, read it aloud two times as you have done on previous days. Use the pointer and stickers to identify periods and capital letters. Using the pointer yourself, read over the sentences once more. Instruct your child to:

- Stand up each time you reach a capital letter at the beginning of the sentence.
- Hop when you reach a capital letter in the middle of a sentence.
- Sit down when you reach a period.

The Writing Project - Article about Insects

For the writing project, your child will write an a article about insects with the information he gathered. His article will need:

- One sentence introducing the article.
- At least three sentences that tell more about the topic (supporting information).
- One sentence that brings the article to an end.

Directions

1. Using the story web and the graphic organizer while you work, write the article on a piece of grade-level writing paper. Skip every other line to allow room for editing and revising.

2. Encourage your child to write independently as much as he can, even if it is only certain alphabet letters, high-frequency words, or simple sentences. Share the pencil back and forth to help a younger student gain confidence until he feels ready to try writing entire sentences on his own.
3. Here is a sample of a completed story.

    Scary Bugs
    Bugs can be scary.
    A beetle is scary because it can run across my toes.
    I was scared when I heard a bee fly by.
    The scariest of all is the big brown spider with eight legs.
    I don't like scary bugs.

Smaller Steps - Making a Portable Word Bank about Insects

For a younger child, follow the instructions in the Pre-writing Activity for Lesson 5 to make a *Portable Word Bank* that lists vocabulary words about bugs. Your student can refer to this as she writes, choosing words from the *Portable Word Bank* to use in her article.

Flying Higher - Writing from an Insect's Point of View

An accelerated or advanced student may enjoy using his imagination to write an article from the insect's point of view.

ACTIVITY SET 8:5

Guided Writing Practice

Write the following predictable sentence starters:

Hello
Today is
It is
We will
I think

At a Glance: Activity Set 8:5

- Guided Writing Practice
- Editing and Revising

Talk about ways to complete each sentence. Write a title at the top.

After your Guided Writing Practice is written on paper, read it aloud two times as you have done on previous days. Use the pointer and stickers to identify periods and capital letters. Using the pointer yourself, read over the sentences once more. Instruct your child to:

- Stand up each time you reach a capital letter at the beginning of the sentence.
- Hop when you reach a capital letter in the middle of a sentence.
- Sit down when you reach a period.

Editing and Revising

Sit down with your child and his Writing Project. Read the story together.

1. Ask:
   - *Does your article have a beginning and an end?*
   - *Does the middle of the article give more information about your bug (or bugs)?*
   - *Does the title express the main idea or tell what your article is about?*

   If not, discuss ideas for improvement.
2. Examine each sentence with your child. Make sure each sentence has an end mark and begins with a capital letter.
3. Ask the child if each sentence makes a complete thought.
4. Help your child write down the changes to his story. Write the corrections on the paper itself.

ACTIVITY SET 8:6

Guided Writing Practice

Write the following predictable sentence starters:

Hello
Today is
It is
We will
I think

At a Glance: Activity Set 8:6

- Guided Writing Practice
- Activity Set Worksheet: "A Web of Ideas"

Talk about ways to complete each sentence. Write a title at the top.

After your Guided Writing Practice is written on paper, read it aloud two times as you have done on previous days. Use the pointer and stickers to identify periods and capital letters. Using the pointer yourself, read over the sentences once more. Instruct your child to:

- Stand up each time you reach a capital letter at the beginning of the sentence.
- Hop when you reach a capital letter in the middle of a sentence.
- Sit down when you reach a period.

Activity Set Worksheet: "A Web of Ideas"

Use Lesson 8: "A Web of Ideas" Activity Set Worksheet.

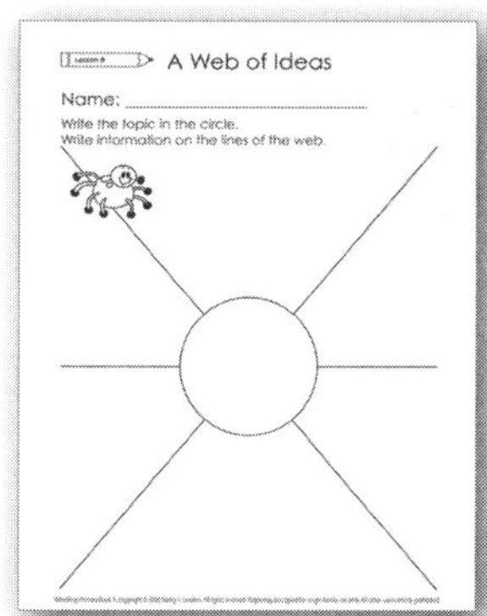

1. Browse through the cards in the Idea Box from Activity Set 3:3. Have your child choose one topic to write about.
2. Write the topic in the circle, and write supporting information on the lines of the web.
3. On the back of the page, encourage your child to draw a picture and practice writing a story all by himself using the information from his story web.
4. Praise your child for his efforts to write a story independently. Do not edit or revise the story because this is just an opportunity for him to practice doing it on his own.

ACTIVITY SET 8:7

Guided Writing Practice

Write the following predictable sentence starters:

Hello
Today is
It is
We will
I think

At a Glance: Activity Set 8:7

- Guided Writing Practice
- Publishing the Project

Talk about ways to complete each sentence. Write a title at the top.

After your Guided Writing Practice is written on paper, read it aloud two times as you have done on previous days. Use the pointer and stickers to identify periods and capital letters. Using the pointer yourself, read over the sentences once more. Instruct your child to:

- Stand up each time you reach a capital letter at the beginning of the sentence.
- Hop when you reach a capital letter in the middle of a sentence.
- Sit down when you reach a period.

Publishing the Project - Making a Giant Caterpillar Pull Toy

Advance Prep

Cut out 4-inch squares of computer or copy paper, one for the title and for each sentence in the completed writing project about bugs.

Help your child publish his article by making it into a giant caterpillar to pull from room to room. Here's how.

1. Together with your child (according to his ability), write one sentence of the story on each square of paper.
2. If there is room, draw a picture for each sentence.
3. Write the title on a separate square of paper.
4. Glue or tape each square of copy paper on the center of a 10-inch paper plate, one sentence per plate.
5. Arrange the plates side by side next to each other so the sentences are in the correct order. Be sure to start with the title.
6. Use a hole punch to punch two holes on opposite sides of each paper plate.

7. Tie each of the plates together side by side with short pieces of yarn to form one long caterpillar.
8. Attach an extra plate at the end of the sentences for the tail of the caterpillar. Have your child write his name on the tail.
9. Attach an extra plate on the opposite end, just in front of the title, and draw a smiley face on it to resemble a caterpillar's face.
10. Use a hole punch to punch one hole at the top of the caterpillar's face. Attach a 2-foot length of yarn through this hole.
11. Encourage your child to pull his caterpillar from room to room, stopping to read his article to everyone he sees.

ACTIVITY SET 8:8

Guided Writing Practice

Write the following predictable sentence starters:

Hello
Today is
It is
We will
I think

At a Glance: Activity Set 8:8

- Guided Writing Practice
- Evaluating the Student's Work
- Want to Do More? (optional) Writing Across the Curriculum: Spotlight on Social Studies

Talk about ways to complete each sentence. Write a title at the top.

After your Guided Writing Practice is written on paper, read it aloud two times as you have done on previous days. Use the pointer and stickers to identify periods and capital letters. Using the pointer yourself, read over the sentences once more. Instruct your child to:

- Stand up each time you reach a capital letter at the beginning of the sentence.
- Hop when you reach a capital letter in the middle of a sentence.
- Sit down when you reach a period.

Evaluating the Student's Work

Use the Primary Writing Skills Evaluation Chart for Lessons 6-10 to evaluate your student's work.

Want to Do More?

Writing Across the Curriculum: Spotlight on Social Studies - Writing an Article about an Historical Person

Help your child create a story web and simple graphic organizer to organize information and article ideas about an historical person she has recently been studying. Here's how.

1. Use the information to write an article about this famous person.
2. When finished writing, create a nearly life-sized paper doll of the person. Lay out two long sheets of butcher paper, one on top of the other. Have your child lie down on top of the butcher paper, and trace the general outline of her whole body.
3. Use crayons or markers to draw clothes on your child's outline and decorate the doll to resemble the famous person.
4. Cut out both sheets of matching butcher paper. Staple the edges together all around the body, stuffing lightly with tissue paper or shredded newspaper as you go.

5. Staple your child's article in the doll's hand so it can easily be read by others.
6. Seat the paper doll in a chair at the writing center. Enjoy the special visitor your child helped to step out from the pages of history!

Lesson 9: Writing from Personal Experience

Lesson Focus: Introducing the Personal Narrative Story
Theme: TV and Movies

Objectives

Your child will:

- Write about something that happened to her.
- Think of ideas to write about from her own experiences.
- Learn to write a personal narrative.
- Practice writing independently as much as possible.

Materials

Guided Writing Practice

- Pointers
- Tablet or chart paper and markers

Pre-writing Activities

- Picture book about the personal experience of a child who is about the same age as yours
- *Story Idea Box* from Activity Set 3:3
- Computer or copy paper
- Crayons or markers

Brainstorming

- Tablet or chart paper and markers

The Writing Project

- Yellow construction or scrapbooking paper
- Pencils or markers

Activity Set Worksheet

- Pencils, crayons, or markers

Publishing the Project

- 9- x 12-inch construction paper
- White butcher paper (or gift wrap with one plain white side)
- Scissors, ruler, clear tape

Want to Do More?

- Writing Across the Curriculum
  - ~ Encyclopedia article, website, or science book about ladybugs
  - ~ Computer or copy paper
  - ~ 10-inch white paper plate
  - ~ Red construction paper
  - ~ Black crayon or marker
  - ~ Pencils, crayons, or markers
  - ~ Metal paper fasteners or brads
  - ~ Scissors, glue
- Computer Capers
  - ~ Digital camera
  - ~ Props to perform a simple play (will vary, depending on the story the child writes for the Writing Project on pages 151-52)

ACTIVITY SET 9:1

Guided Writing Practice

Write the following predictable sentence starters:

Hello
Today is
It is
We are going to
I feel

At a Glance: Activity Set 9:1

- Guided Writing Practice
- Pre-writing Activity (optional)

Because your child will be writing a personal narrative for the Writing Project, guide him to complete these sentence starters by thinking about and describing upcoming activities for each day. Discuss various options for ideas on how to complete each of the five sentences. Here's one idea.

You: *Whom should we say hello to this morning?*

Child: Blackie.

You: *Hello, Blackie. Let's write that down.*

You: *Now let's look at the calendar. What day is today?*

Child: Tuesday.

You: *Good. Today is Tuesday. Say that. "Today is Tuesday."*

Child: Today is Tuesday.

You: *You're right! What can we say about today?*

Child: It's Grant's birthday!

You: *Yes, it's Grant's birthday! Say that. "It is Grant's birthday."*

Child: It is Grant's birthday.

You: *It is Grant's birthday. Good! Let's write that down.*

You: *So. . .what are we going to do today?*

Child: We're going to have a party!

You: *Yes, we are! Let's write that down. We are going to have a party.*

You: *How do you feel about that?*

Child: Excited!

You: *Why do you feel excited?*

Child: Because we get to have birthday cake.

You: *I feel excited because we will have birthday cake. Say that. "I feel excited because we will have birthday cake."*

Child: I feel excited because we will have birthday cake.

You: What a great story! Let's choose our pointers and read it together.

Hello, Blackie.
Today is Tuesday.
It is Grant's birthday.
We are going to have a party.
I feel excited because we will have birthday cake.

Encourage your child to write as many letters or words as he can. When the sentences are finished, ask him to help choose a title. Write the title at the top.

After your Guided Writing Practice is written on paper, read it aloud two times. Here's how:

1. Using a pointer yourself, read over the sentences together. At the end of each sentence, point to the period and pause before going on.
2. Ask your child to choose a pointer to point to each word as you once more read the sentences together.
3. Use the pointer yourself to read over the sentences again. Read the sentences slowly to give time for your child to respond. Instruct your child to:
   - Stand up each time you reach a capital letter at the beginning of the sentence.
   - Hop when you reach a capital letter in the middle of a sentence.
   - Sit down when you reach a period.

You will use the same predictable sentence starters every day of Lesson 9.

Pre-writing Activity (optional) - Word Family Flowers

If time permits sometime during Lesson 9, make another word family flower or add new words to existing flowers in your *Garden of Rhyming Words* notebook. This notebook will provide a handy reference in Lesson 4 of Book B when you teach your child to write a poem or nursery rhyme. You will also find this notebook handy any time your child writes with rhyme.

If your child has not yet made a *Garden of Rhyming Words* notebook, see Activity Set 7:2 for instructions and a list of word families.

ACTIVITY SET 9:2

Guided Writing Practice

Write the following predictable sentence starters:

Hello
Today is
It is
We are going to
I feel

> **At a Glance: Activity Set 9:2**
> - Guided Writing Practice
> - Pre-writing Activities: Picture book about a child's experience

Because your child will be writing a personal narrative for the Writing Project, guide her to complete these sentence starters by thinking about and describing upcoming activities for each day. Discuss various options for ideas on how to complete each of the five sentences.

Encourage your child to write as many letters or words as she can. When the sentences are finished, ask her to help choose a title. Write the title at the top. Here is an example of a completed Guided Writing Practice.

Reading is Fun with Friends
Hello, friend.
Today is Monday.
It is the first day of the month of May.
We are going to read our favorite books together.
I feel happy because I like to read!

After your Guided Writing Practice is written on paper, read it aloud two times as you have done on previous days. Using the pointer yourself, read over the sentences once more. Instruct your child to:

- Stand up each time you reach a capital letter at the beginning of the sentence.
- Hop when you reach a capital letter in the middle of a sentence.
- Sit down when you reach a period.

Pre-writing Activities

Picture Book about a Child's Experience
Choose a picture book to read to your child about the personal experience of a child who is about the same age as yours.

Choosing a Topic
For the writing project, your child will be writing a personal narrative.

1. Help her use the file box of *Story Ideas* that you made during Activity Set 3:3 to choose four potential topics to write about. Each of these topics should be about something your child

actually did. For instance, if she chooses an index card about basketball, she will write about a time she played basketball at the park or watched a basketball game on TV with her grandpa.

2. If your child wants to write about topics that aren't in the file box, help her make a new index card for each idea by drawing or gluing a picture on the front and writing the label on the back. Add the new cards to the file box.
3. Help your child fold a paper into four equal spaces. Have her write the four topics she chose, one in each space of the paper. In each of the corresponding spaces, she can draw a picture about what she might like to write about for each of the topics. Each picture should represent a memory of her own personal experience.
4. When she is finished, have your child choose one of the ideas she would like to write about.

ACTIVITY SET 9:3

Guided Writing Practice

Write the following predictable sentence starters:

> *Hello*
> *Today is*
> *It is*
> *We are going to*
> *I feel*

At a Glance: Activity Set 9:3

- Guided Writing Practice
- Brainstorming
- Smaller Steps

Talk about ways to complete each sentence. When finished, ask him to help choose a title. Write the title at the top. Here is an example.

> <u>A Week at the Beach</u>
> Hello, Mom.
> Today is Thursday.
> It is almost vacation time.
> We are going to the beach for a whole week!
> I feel like taking my sand toys.

After your Guided Writing Practice is written on paper, read it aloud two times as you have done on previous days. Using the pointer yourself, read over the sentences once more. Instruct your child to:

- Stand up each time you reach a capital letter at the beginning of the sentence.
- Hop when you reach a capital letter in the middle of a sentence.
- Sit down when you reach a period.

Brainstorming - Using a Story Web and a Graphic Organizer

Directions

1. Sitting with your child, draw a simple story web on paper with a circle in the middle and five or six lines extending out from the circle to resemble a spider's web.
2. In the center of the circle, write the topic your child has chosen.
3. On each of the lines, list information that supports the topic. Write one word or one sentence on each line representing something your child remembers about his experience.
4. On a separate piece of paper, make a simple graphic organizer to list ideas for the beginning, middle, and ending of your child's upcoming writing project. Your child will be writing a personal narrative. Therefore, label the graphic organizer as follows, leaving spaces for writing as you brainstorm together:

Title:
Introduction:
Body:
Closing:

5. Discuss possible introductions. Write these sentences on the graphic organizer.
6. Look at the story web with your child to choose at least three nuggets of supporting information to include in the body of the writing project. Write these on the graphic organizer.
7. Discuss possible closings. Write these sentences on the graphic organizer.
8. Brainstorm possible titles and write these on the graphic organizer.

Smaller Steps - Building Confidence in a Young Writer

To build confidence in a younger or reluctant writer, write simple sentences on the story web during the brainstorming session. He can then copy these sentences down during the Writing Project.

ACTIVITY SET 9:4

Guided Writing Practice

Write the following predictable sentence starters:

Hello
Today is
It is
We are going to
I feel

At a Glance: Activity Set 9:4

Guided Writing Practice
The Writing Project
Smaller Steps or Flying Higher

Talk about ways to complete each sentence. When finished, ask him to help choose a title. Write the title at the top. Here is an example.

A Bad Day
Hello, Papa.
Today is Friday.
It is raining very hard.
We are going to get hair cuts after Kyle's nap.
I feel like this will be a bad day.

After your Guided Writing Practice is written on paper, read it aloud two times as you have done on previous days. Using the pointer yourself, read over the sentences once more. Instruct your child to:

- Stand up each time you reach a capital letter at the beginning of the sentence.
- Hop when you reach a capital letter in the middle of a sentence.
- Sit down when you reach a period.

The Writing Project - Personal Experience Story

Advance Prep

Cut out at least five large stars from yellow construction paper, big enough for your child to write one sentence on each star.

For the writing project, your child will write a personal experience story. He will write one sentence introducing the story, at least three sentences with supporting information, and one sentence as a closing.

Directions

1. Explain that your child is the "star of the show" when he writes a personal narrative.
2. Using the story web and the graphic organizer while you work, guide your child to write his story on the paper stars, one sentence per star. Number the stars to keep the sentences in order.
3. Encourage your child to write independently as much as he can, even if it is only certain alphabet letters, high-frequency words, or simple sentences. Share the pencil back and forth to help younger students gain confidence until they feel ready to try writing entire words or sentences on their own.
4. Here is a sample of a completed story.

    My Sandwich
    Last summer I went to the beach.
    We had a picnic with peanut butter and jelly sandwiches.
    I put my sandwich down on my napkin to eat a piece of watermelon.
    A seagull took my sandwich.
    He flew away and dropped it in the sand.
    Now it was a sandy sandwich!

Smaller Steps - Copying Sentences

During the brainstorming session, your younger or reluctant child may have dictated sentences for you to write on his story web. If so, he can now copy these sentences down on the yellow paper stars.

Flying Higher - Adding Ingredients to a Narrative

Challenge an accelerated or advanced student to add a variety of ingredients to her personal narrative such as humor, rhyme, or an especially descriptive word.

ACTIVITY SET 9:5

Guided Writing Practice

Write the following predictable sentence starters:

Hello
Today is
It is
We are going to
I feel

At a Glance: Activity Set 9:5

- Guided Writing Practice
- Editing and Revising

When the sentences are finished, ask him to help choose a title. Write the title at the top.

After your Guided Writing Practice is written on paper, read it aloud two times as you have done on previous days. Using the pointer yourself, read over the sentences once more. Instruct your child to:

- Stand up each time you reach a capital letter at the beginning of the sentence.
- Hop when you reach a capital letter in the middle of a sentence.
- Sit down when you reach a period.

Editing and Revising

Sit down with your child and her Writing Project story. Read the story together.

1. Discuss the structure of the story. Ask, "Does your story have a beginning, supporting information in the middle, and an end?" and "Does the title express the main idea?" If not, discuss ideas for improvement.
2. Examine each sentence with your child. Make sure each sentence has an end mark and begins with a capital letter.
3. Ask the child if each sentence makes a complete thought.
4. Help your child write down the changes to her story. Write the corrections on each star itself.

ACTIVITY SET 9:6

Guided Writing Practice

Write the following predictable sentence starters:

Hello
Today is
It is
We are going to
I feel

> **At a Glance: Activity Set 9:6**
> - Guided Writing Practice
> - Activity Set Worksheet: "On With the Show!"

When the sentences are finished, ask him to help choose a title. Write the title at the top.

After your Guided Writing Practice is written on paper, read it aloud two times as you have done on previous days. Using the pointer yourself, read over the sentences once more. Instruct your child to:

- Stand up each time you reach a capital letter at the beginning of the sentence.
- Hop when you reach a capital letter in the middle of a sentence.
- Sit down when you reach a period.

Activity Set Worksheet: "On With the Show!"

Use Lesson 9: "On With the Show!" Activity Set Worksheet.

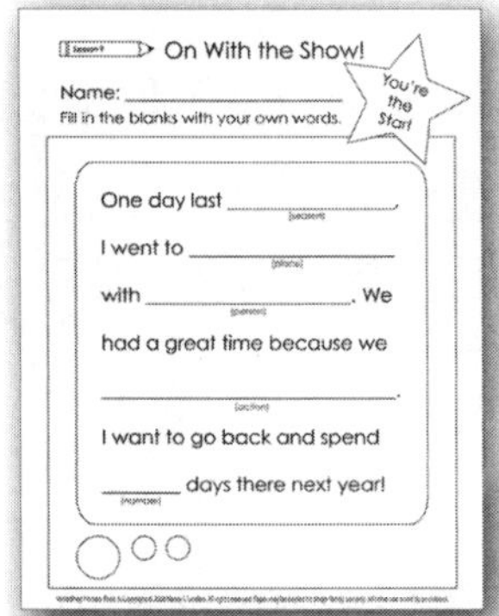

On With the Show!

Name: ____________

Fill in the blanks with your own words.

You're the Star!

One day last ____________.

I went to ____________

with ____________. We

had a great time because we

____________.

I want to go back and spend

______ days there next year!

1. Read over the sentences on the worksheet with your child. Discuss possible words to write in the blanks.
2. Have your child fill in the blanks about something she remembers doing.
3. On the back of the page, encourage your child to draw a picture and write about her memory all by herself.
4. Praise your child for her efforts to write independently. Do not edit or revise the story because this is just an opportunity for her to practice doing it on her own.

ACTIVITY SET 9:7

Guided Writing Practice

Write the following predictable sentence starters:

Hello
Today is
It is
We are going to
I feel

At a Glance: Activity Set 9:7

- Guided Writing Practice
- Publishing the Project

When the sentences are finished, ask him to help choose a title. Write the title at the top.

After your Guided Writing Practice is written on paper, read it aloud two times as you have done on previous days. Using the pointer yourself, read over the sentences once more. Instruct your child to:

- Stand up each time you reach a capital letter at the beginning of the sentence.
- Hop when you reach a capital letter in the middle of a sentence.
- Sit down when you reach a period.

Publishing the Project - Making a TV Movie

Advance Prep

- Use a piece of 9- x 12-inch construction paper to make a TV. Measure in two inches from each side of the paper TV.
- Starting about one inch down from the top edge and stopping one inch above the bottom edge, cut a 6-inch slit from top to bottom, one slit on the right and one on the left. (Use a stiff piece of cardboard, poster board, or tag board if you choose to make the TV sturdier.)
- Cut a 5½- x 36-inch strip of white butcher paper or gift wrap that has a plain white side. Allowing three inches at each end, mark off three 10-inch sections on the white paper strip.

Turn your child's personal experience story into a TV "movie." Here's how.

1. Starting at the left edge, help your child write and illustrate her story on the white paper strip. Her story will be divided into three sections, with a picture and one or more sentences in each section. Be sure to include the title at the top of the first section.
2. Feed the paper through the slots of the paper TV. When it is centered in the TV, fold back both edges of extra space on the white paper strip. Tape the edges to form handles. Practice pulling

the strip back and forth by the handles to tell the story.

3. Gather your family together for a special "movie" premier. Pop popcorn, sit on comfy chairs, and watch your child share her very own "movie." Lights! Camera! Action!

ACTIVITY SET 9:8

Guided Writing Practice

Write the following predictable sentence starters:

Hello
Today is
It is
We are going to
I feel

When the sentences are finished, ask him to help choose a title. Write the title at the top.

After your Guided Writing Practice is written on paper, read it aloud two times as you have done on previous days.
Using the pointer yourself, read over the sentences once more. Instruct your child to:

- Stand up each time you reach a capital letter at the beginning of the sentence.
- Hop when you reach a capital letter in the middle of a sentence.
- Sit down when you reach a period.

At a Glance: Activity Set 9:8

- Guided Writing Practice
- Evaluating the Student's Work
- Want to Do More? (optional) Writing Across the Curriculum: Spotlight on Science
- Want to Do More? (optional) Computer Capers

Evaluating the Student's Work

Use the Primary Writing Skills Evaluation Chart for Lessons 6-10 to evaluate your student's work.

Want to Do More?

Writing Across the Curriculum: Spotlight on Science - Ladybug Story and Craft
Directions

1. Use an encyclopedia, the Internet, or nature book to read about ladybugs. Write down interesting facts or observations.
2. Have your child pretend to be a ladybug and write a five-sentence personal experience story from the viewpoint of the ladybug. Write the story on a 6-inch square of white computer or copy paper.
3. Glue the story on the top side of a white 10-inch paper plate, as far down toward the bottom edge as possible.
4. Cut out two ladybug wings from red construction paper just large enough to completely cover the story. Use a crayon or black marker to decorate the wings with matching black spots.
5. Mount the two wings on the paper plate with a metal paper fastener or brad. Put one brad at the top left corner of the left wing and one brad at the top right corner of the right wing, so

that the wings open to reveal the story underneath.

6. Use red and black crayons or markers to draw the ladybug's face on the paper plate just above the wings.

Computer Capers - Creating a Photo Slideshow

Directions

1. Take a series of digital pictures with your child performing her story as a play. Be sure to dress up in costumes, use fun props, and decorate the background.
2. Include a picture of your child holding the title of the story written in large letters on a piece of paper.
3. Use the photo slideshow feature on your computer to create a slideshow of your child's play.
4. As you watch the slideshow together, read your child's story aloud.

Lesson 10: Sequence of Events

Lesson Focus: Writing About Events in the Order They Happen
Theme: Cars and Trucks

Objectives

Your child will:

- Use order words to describe a sequence of events.
- Write about the order of events in her own day.
- Identify punctuation marks such as question marks and exclamation points.
- Organize a story according to its sequence of events.
- Write standard spelling of high-frequency vocabulary words.

Materials

Guided Writing Practice

- Pointers
- Tablet or chart paper and markers

Pre-writing Activities

- *My Garden of Rhyming Words* notebook from Activity Set 7:2
    - ~ Construction or scrapbooking paper in a variety of solid colors, including green
    - ~ White computer or copy paper
    - ~ Scissors, hole punch, markers, glue
- Picture storybook about a vehicle such as a dump truck, a school bus, or a race car (choose a book with a story, not a book of facts)
- Crayons or markers
- Scissors

Brainstorming

- Butcher paper or a solid-color sheet of gift wrap
- Tablet or chart paper
- Computer or copy paper
- Writing paper
- Scissors
- Pencils, crayons, or markers

The Writing Project

- Unlined or lined writing paper
- Pencils or markers
- Scissors

Activity Set Worksheet

- Pencils, scissors
- Crayons or markers, including green, yellow, and red

Publishing the Project

- 9- x 12-inch construction paper, including black
- White chalk or crayon
- Glue, clear tape, scissors
- Toy car

Want to Do More?

- Writing Across the Curriculum
  - ~ Encyclopedia, Internet access, or a science book about watermelons
  - ~ 12- x 18-inch construction paper, including pink and green
  - ~ Blank index cards
  - ~ Black marker or crayon
  - ~ Crayons, pencils, or markers
  - ~ Scissors, glue, tape
  - ~ Optional: watermelon seeds and planting materials

ACTIVITY SET 10:1

Guided Writing Practice

Write the following predictable sentence starters. Skip a space between each line to allow room for extra sentences.

> *Today is*
> *First, we will*
> *Next, we are going to*
> *Last of all, we will*
> *I think*

At a Glance: Activity Set 10:1

- Guided Writing Practice
- Pre-writing Activity (optional)

Talk with your child about the upcoming schedule for today. Discuss various options for ideas on how to complete each of the five sentences. Encourage adding additional sentences to the text that use punctuation such as question marks and exclamation points.

Be sure to list the events of the day in their correct order. For the last sentence, write a conclusion about the day's upcoming activities.

Encourage your child to write as many letters or words as he can. When the sentences are finished, ask him to help choose a title. Write the title at the top. Here's one idea.

You: *We have a busy day ahead of us! Let's look at the calendar. What day is today?*

Child: Today is Monday.

You: *You're right! Thank you for using a complete sentence. What is the first thing we plan to do today?*

Child: Math.

You: *Whoops! Remember to use a complete sentence, okay? First, we will do math. Say that. "First, we will do math."*

Child: First, we will do math.

You: *Good! Here's the marker. Can you write "do math" by yourself?*

Child: Yes!

You: *Good job. Now, tell me...what are you learning to do in math?*

Child: I am learning to subtract.

You: *Super! Let's write that down. I am learning to subtract.*

You: *After math, what are we going to do next?*

Child: Next we are going to check our science experiment.

You: *Let's share the marker. Help me write some of those words, okay?*

You: *What will we do last of all?*

Child: Have art?

You: That's right. Do you remember what we will use for art? Try that as a complete sentence. Last of all, _____.

Child: Last of all, we will use clay for art.

You: And what do you think about playing with clay?

Child: I can't wait!

You: So we can write: Last of all we will use clay for art. I can't wait.

You: Do you know what kind of punctuation mark shows that you are excited?

Child: No.

You: An exclamation point. Let's put one after "I can't wait!"

You: Now you need to finish your story with a sentence that brings everything to an end. Your last sentence will begin with "I think." So, when you look at ALL the things you will do today, you can finish your story by saying: "I think _____."

Child: I think I will be very busy today.

You: I agree! All that's left is a title. Any ideas?

Child: Our Busy Day?

You: That works! Let's choose our pointers and read your story together.

Our Busy Day
Today is Tuesday.
First, we will do math. I am learning to subtract.
Next, we are going to check our science experiment.
Last of all, we will use clay for art. I can't wait!
I think I will be very busy today.

After your Guided Writing Practice is written on paper, read it aloud two times. Here's how:

1. Using a pointer yourself, read over the sentences together. At the end of each sentence, point to the period and pause before going on.
2. Ask your child to choose a pointer to point to each word as you once more read the sentences together.
3. Use the pointer yourself to read over the sentences again. Read the sentences slowly to give time for your child to respond. Instruct your child to:
   - Stand up each time you reach a capital letter at the beginning of the sentence.
   - Hop when you reach a capital letter in the middle of a sentence.
   - Sit down when you reach a period.

You will use the same predictable sentence starters every day of Lesson 10.

Pre-writing Activity (optional) - Word Family Flowers

If time permits sometime during Lesson 10, make another word family flower or add new words to existing flowers in your *Garden of Rhyming Words* notebook. This notebook will provide a handy reference in Lesson 4 of Book B when you teach your child to write a poem or nursery rhyme. You will also find this notebook handy any time your child writes with rhyme.

If your child has not yet made a *Garden of Rhyming Words* notebook, see Activity Set 7:2 for instructions and a list of word families.

ACTIVITY SET 10:2

Guided Writing Practice

Write the following predictable sentence starters. Skip a space between each line to allow room for extra sentences.

> *Today is*
> *First, we will*
> *Next, we are going to*
> *Last of all, we will*
> *I think*

At a Glance: Activity Set 10:2

- Guided Writing Practice
- Pre-writing Activities: Picture book with a story about a vehicle

Talk with your child about the upcoming schedule for today. Discuss various options for ideas on how to complete each of the five sentences. Encourage adding additional sentences to the text that use punctuation such as question marks and exclamation points.

Point out the order words that help organize the story: *First*, *next*, and *last of all*. Be sure to list the events of the day in their correct order. For the last sentence, write a conclusion about the day's upcoming activities.

Encourage your child to write as many letters or words as he can. When the sentences are finished, ask him to help choose a title. Write the title at the top. Here's an example of a completed Guided Writing Practice.

> Errand Day
> Today is Wednesday.
> First, we will finish our schoolwork.
> Next, we are going to the post office.
> Last of all, we will go to the grocery store. Can I get a special treat?
> I think I will be tired when we get home.

After your Guided Writing Practice is written on paper, read it aloud two times. Here's how.

1. Using a pointer yourself, read over the sentences together. At the end of each sentence, point to the period and pause before going on.
2. Ask your child to choose a pointer to point to each word as you once more read the sentences.
3 Use the pointer yourself to read over the sentences again. Read the sentences slowly to give time for your child to respond. Instruct your child to:
   - Stand up each time you reach a capital letter at the beginning of the sentence.
   - Hop when you reach a capital letter in the middle of a sentence.
   - Sit down when you reach a period.

Pre-writing Activities

Picture Book about a Vehicle

Choose a picture storybook about a vehicle such as a dump truck, school bus, or race car to read to your child. Make sure it's a story, not a nonfiction book of facts.

Putting Events in Order

Directions

1. Discuss the order of key events in the story. Use order words such as *first, second, third* or *next, then, finally,* and *last.*
2. On a piece of chart paper or tablet, list the sequence of 3-5 key events from the book in their correct order, skipping a line between each event. For pre-readers, draw a simple picture to represent each event.
3. Cut apart the list so each event is on a separate slip of paper. You should have 3-5 slips of paper.
4. Hide the slips of paper throughout the room. (Don't let your child peek!)
5. Have your child find all the slips of paper.
6. Help your child place the slips of paper in order to arrange the events as they happened from the beginning to the end of the story. Ask, "What happened *first*?" or "What happened *next*?"
7. Read the picture book to your child again to check her work. Work together to rearrange the slips of paper in the correct sequence if a mistake was made.

ACTIVITY SET 10:3

Guided Writing Practice

Write the following predictable sentence starters. Skip a space between each line to allow room for extra sentences.

> *Today is*
> *First, we will*
> *Next, we are going to*
> *Last of all, we will*
> *I think*

At a Glance: Activity Set 10:3

- Guided Writing Practice
- Brainstorming

Talk with your child about the upcoming schedule for today. Discuss various options for ideas on how to complete each of the five sentences. Encourage adding additional sentences to the text that use punctuation such as question marks and exclamation points.

Point out the order words that help organize the story: *First*, *next*, and *last of all*. Be sure to list the events of the day in their correct order. For the last sentence, write a conclusion about the day's upcoming activities.

Encourage your child to write as many letters or words as he can. When the sentences are finished, ask him to help choose a title. Write the title at the top. Here's an example of a completed Guided Writing Practice.

> A Fun Friday
> Today is Friday.
> First, we will do chores. I want to fold the towels.
> Next, we are going to play some games.
> Last of all, we will eat dinner. I hope you're making spaghetti!
> I think today will be a fun Friday.

After your Guided Writing Practice is written on paper, read it aloud two times as you have done on previous days. Using the pointer yourself, read over the sentences once more. Instruct your child to:

- Stand up each time you reach a capital letter at the beginning of the sentence.
- Hop when you reach a capital letter in the middle of a sentence.
- Sit down when you reach a period.

Brainstorming - Organizing the Sequence of Events

Advance Prep

Use butcher paper or a solid-color sheet of gift wrap to cut out a large paper shape of a car or truck.

For the writing project, your child will write a story about a vehicle such as a car, truck, cement mixer, or bus. Brainstorming will help him think about how to organize his thoughts and ideas. Here's how:

1. Help your child fold a piece of unlined paper into four equal spaces. In each space, have him draw a picture of a vehicle he might want to write about. In each corresponding space, help him write a sentence about a potential story involving that vehicle. Use ideas from the picture book you read together or think of new ones.
2. When he is finished, encourage him to choose which of the four topics he wants to write about for the writing project.
3. On the large paper shape of a car or truck, make a simple graphic organizer to list ideas for the beginning, middle, and ending of your child's story. Label the graphic organizer as follows, leaving spaces for writing as you brainstorm together:

   Title:
   Beginning:
   Middle:
   Ending:
4. Discuss possible beginnings. Write these sentences on the graphic organizer.
5. Discuss how your child wants the story to progress. Talk about the sequence of the events. Prompt him with questions. Use order words to ask questions such as, "What happened *first*?" (*First*, the big bus grew wings.) Ask, "What happened *next*?" (*Next*, everyone got on the bus.) Ask, "*Then* what happened?" (*Then*, the bus flew through the sky.) Ask, "What happened *last of all*?" (*Finally*, it flew home.)
6. Write at least three sentences on the graphic organizer listing the sequence of events in the middle of the story.
7. Talk about potential endings. Write these sentences on the graphic organizer.
8. Brainstorm potential titles and write these on the graphic organizer.

ACTIVITY SET 10:4

Guided Writing Practice

Write the following predictable sentence starters. Skip a space between each line to allow room for extra sentences.

Today is
First, we will
Next, we are going to
Last of all, we will
I think

At a Glance: Activity Set 10:4

- Guided Writing Practice
- The Writing Project
- Smaller Steps or Flying Higher

Directions

1. Talk with your child about your plans for the day.
2. List the events of the day in their correct order.
3. As you complete the sentences together, encourage use of punctuation such as question marks and exclamation points.
4. When the sentences are finished, choose a title together. Write the title at the top. Here's an example:

    Book Night
    Today is Monday.
    First, we will go to the park. Nathan will be there too.
    Next, we are going to the library.
    Last of all, we will read books with Dad. That's my favorite part!
    I think tonight will be book night.

Read the sentences aloud two times as you have done on previous days. Using the pointer yourself, read over the sentences once more. Instruct your child to:

- Stand up each time you reach a capital letter at the beginning of the sentence.
- Hop when you reach a capital letter in the middle of a sentence.
- Sit down when you reach a period.

The Writing Project - Story about a Vehicle

Advance Prep

Cut unlined or lined writing paper into 6-inch squares.

Directions

1. Using the graphic organizer while you work, guide your child to write her story on the 6-inch squares, using as many order words as possible such as *first*, *second*, *third*, *next*, and *finally*. Have her write one event on each square of paper.
2. Be sure to leave enough space between each line for making corrections during revision.
3. Encourage your child to write independently as much as she can, even if it is only certain alphabet letters, high-frequency words, or simple sentences. Share the pencil back and forth to help younger students gain confidence until they feel ready to try writing entire sentences on their own.

Smaller Steps - Practicing with Sequence Words

Help a younger learner grasp the concept of sequence of events. Here's how:

1. Cut out 3-inch shapes of the numbers 1-5 from construction paper.
2. Lay out the numbers in correct order on the table.
    - Point to the number 1. Ask what happened *first.*
    - Point to the number 2. Ask what happened *second.*
    - Point to the number 3. Ask what happened *third.*
    - Point to the number 4 and ask what happened *next.*
    - Point to the number 5 and ask what happened *finally.*

Flying Higher - Writing a Movie Review

An accelerated or advanced student may enjoy watching a favorite video with you.

1. Pause the video at key points of the story to write down a description of each main event on a simple graphic organizer.
2. When the movie is over, encourage her to use the graphic organizer as a guide to write a movie review describing the events in the order that they occurred.

ACTIVITY SET 10:5

Guided Writing Practice

Write the following predictable sentence starters. Skip a space between each line to allow room for extra sentences.

> *Today is*
> *First, we will*
> *Next, we are going to*
> *Last of all, we will*
> *I think*

At a Glance: Activity Set 10:5

- Guided Writing Practice
- Editing and Revising

Directions

1. Talk with your child about your plans for the day.
2. List the events of the day in their correct order.
3. As you complete the sentences together, encourage use of punctuation such as question marks and exclamation points.
4. When the sentences are finished, choose a title together. Write the title at the top.

Read the sentences aloud two times as you have done on previous days. Using the pointer yourself, read over the sentences once more. Instruct your child to:

- Stand up each time you reach a capital letter at the beginning of the sentence.
- Hop when you reach a capital letter in the middle of a sentence.
- Sit down when you reach a period.

Editing and Revising - Introducing Editing Buddies

Advance Prep

Gather several "editing buddies" to help your child enjoy the editing process more. Keep several small stuffed animals at the writing center. You could store them in:

- A basket or plastic tub.
- A pocket in the backpack of your portable writing center.
- An over-the-door shoe organizer.

Ask your child to select an editing buddy from her new collection. Sit down with your child and her Writing Project story. Read the story aloud to the editing buddy.

1. Discuss the structure of the story. Ask, "Does your story have a beginning, a middle, and an

end?" "Does the title express the main idea?" If not, discuss ideas for improvement.

2. Identify the order words your child used.
3. Talk together about the story's order of events. Ask, "Did you write the events in the order in which they happened?" If not, discuss how to rearrange the sentences.
4. Examine each sentence with your child. Make sure each sentence has an end mark and begins with a capital letter.
5. Check the spelling of high-frequency vocabulary words your child should know such as *the*, *and*, *or*, and her name. Help your child write the standard spelling of these vocabulary words if any of these are spelled incorrectly.
6. Help your child write down the changes to her story.
7. Write the corrections on the paper itself.
8. If your child wants to, help her rewrite the story on new squares of paper.

ACTIVITY SET 10:6

Guided Writing Practice

Write the following predictable sentence starters. Skip a space between each line to allow room for extra sentences.

Today is
First, we will
Next, we are going to
Last of all, we will
I think

At a Glance: Activity Set 10:6

- Guided Writing Practice
- Activity Set Worksheet: "What Comes Next?"

Directions

1. Talk with your child about your plans for the day.
2. List the events of the day in their correct order.
3. As you complete the sentences together, encourage use of punctuation such as question marks and exclamation points.
4. When the sentences are finished, choose a title together. Write the title at the top.

Read the sentences aloud two times as you have done on previous days. Using the pointer yourself, read over the sentences once more. Instruct your child to:

- Stand up each time you reach a capital letter at the beginning of the sentence.
- Hop when you reach a capital letter in the middle of a sentence.
- Sit down when you reach a period.

Activity Set Worksheet: "What Comes Next?"

Use Lesson 10: "What Comes Next?" Activity Set Worksheet.

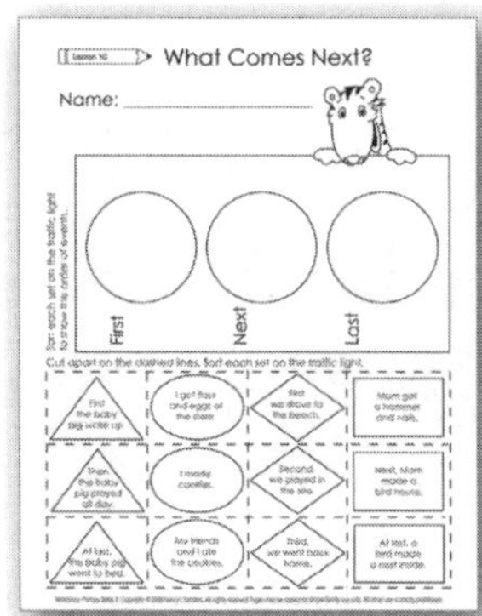

1. Help your child cut out the set of cards at the bottom of the page.
2. Color the traffic light green, yellow, and red. Explain: *First*, the story starts. *Next*, you wait and read what happens. *Last*, the story stops.
3. Sort each set of cards by placing them on the traffic light to show the correct order of events.
4. On the back of the page, have your child practice writing independently about the sequence of events on a topic that interests him.
5. Praise your child for his efforts to write independently. Do not edit or revise the story because this is just an opportunity for him to practice doing it on his own.

ACTIVITY SET 10:7

Guided Writing Practice

Write the following predictable sentence starters. Skip a space between each line to allow room for extra sentences.

Today is
First, we will
Next, we are going to
Last of all, we will
I think

At a Glance: Activity Set 10:7

- Guided Writing Practice
- Publishing the Project

Directions

1. Talk with your child about your plans for the day.
2. List the events of the day in their correct order.
3. As you complete the sentences together, encourage use of punctuation such as question marks and exclamation points.
4. When the sentences are finished, choose a title together. Write the title at the top.

Read the sentences aloud two times as you have done on previous days. Using the pointer yourself, read over the sentences once more. Instruct your child to:

- Stand up each time you reach a capital letter at the beginning of the sentence.
- Hop when you reach a capital letter in the middle of a sentence.
- Sit down when you reach a period.

Publishing the Project - Making a Story Road

Advance Prep

1. Cut out a car or truck shape from 9- x 12-inch construction paper.
2. Use clear tape to tape black sheets of 9- x 12-inch construction paper end to end to form a road long enough to showcase your child's story.
3. Use white chalk or crayon to draw dashed lines along the road.

Your child will publish his project by driving down "Story Road." Here's how.

1. Tape or glue your child's story (the 6-inch squares of paper) on the road. Going from left to right, be sure to place the pieces of paper in the correct order according to the story's sequence of events.

2. Have your child illustrate the car or truck and draw a picture of himself driving. Write his name and tape the vehicle to the far right of the road.
3. Lay your child's published story down on a table or the floor. Invite a family member or friend to read the story. For added fun, drive a toy car slowly along the road from left to right as the story is read aloud.

ACTIVITY SET 10:8

Guided Writing Practice

Write the following predictable sentence starters. Skip a space between each line to allow room for extra sentences.

Today is
First, we will
Next, we are going to
Last of all, we will
I think

At a Glance: Activity Set 10:8

- Guided Writing Practice
- Evaluating the Student's Work
- Want to Do More? (optional) Writing Across the Curriculum: Spotlight on Science

Directions

1. Talk with your child about your plans for the day.
2. List the events of the day in their correct order.
3. As you complete the sentences together, encourage use of punctuation such as question marks and exclamation points.
4. When the sentences are finished, choose a title together. Write the title at the top.

Read the sentences aloud two times as you have done on previous days. Using the pointer yourself, read over the sentences once more. Instruct your child to:

- Stand up each time you reach a capital letter at the beginning of the sentence.
- Hop when you reach a capital letter in the middle of a sentence.
- Sit down when you reach a period.

Evaluating the Student's Work

Use the Primary Writing Skills Progress Chart for Lessons 6-10 to evaluate your student's work.

Want to Do More?

Writing Across the Curriculum: Spotlight on Science - How Does a Watermelon Grow?

Advance Prep

Cut a 12- x 18-inch sheet of green construction paper in half lengthwise to form about a 6- x 18-inch strip.

Help your child write a story about how a watermelon grows. Here's how:

1. Use an encyclopedia, the Internet, or a science book to read about how a watermelon grows.
2. Identify 7 steps for growing a watermelon such as: *Pick a spot in the garden, dig a hole, plant the seed, water the seed, watch the sprout grow, let the sun shine on the plant*, and *pick the watermelon.*
3. Help your child write each of the 7 steps on the blank index cards and add small illustrations.
4. Fold the green construction paper strip by bringing each end of the strip to the middle front and making a crease on each side to form two flaps that meet in the center.
5. Open the flaps. Glue or tape the index cards along the inside of the paper strip in order from left to right so that two cards are inside the left flap, three are across the middle, and two are inside the right flap.

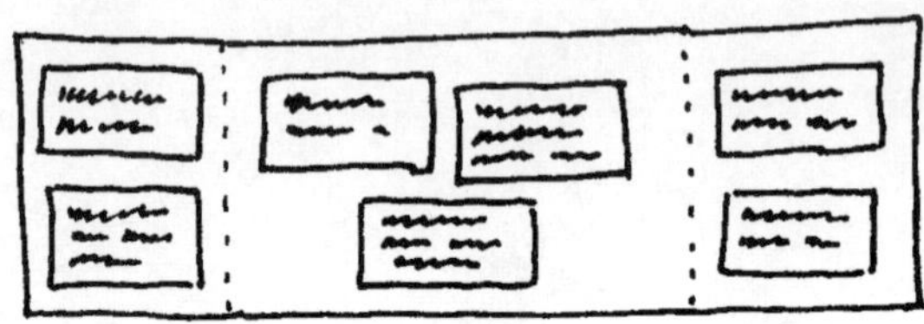

6. Close the flaps. Using pink and green construction paper, help your child make a big slice of watermelon in the shape of an oblong semi-circle to decorate the front of the project. Use a black marker to draw watermelon seeds on the pink part.
7. Cut the slice of watermelon in half so that one half fits on the front of the left flap and one fits on the front of the right flap. Glue or tape the watermelon slice to the front of the flaps so that when the flaps are closed together in the middle, it looks like one big slice of watermelon.

8. Add the title to the front of the project: "How to Grow a Watermelon."
9. Open the flaps and review the steps it takes to grow a watermelon.
10. For extra fun, plant a watermelon seed to observe if your steps are correct!

Master Supply List

A general list of storage suggestions, materials, and supplies for equipping your Writing Center can be found in the Introduction. In addition, the beginning of each lesson includes a list of materials needed specifically for that assignment.

If your Writing Center is well equipped (see pp. 9-11), you should already have most items on hand. Sometimes you'll need something extra, such as a specific color of construction paper, craft sticks, or a zip-top sandwich bag, so it's a good idea to gather these extra supplies in advance so you're not scrambling at the last minute. Below you will find a master list of materials needed for the entire scope of Book A to help you plan ahead. See the Introduction for detailed explanations.

General Writing Center Supplies

Chart Paper or Newsprint Pad

- Chart paper comes lined or unlined and is spiral-bound for easy turning. Typically, chart paper is 2-hole punched with stiff covers for hanging or setting on an easel.
- Newsprint pads or tablets come in various sizes. Though they are usually unlined, you can also find lined ones. Depending on the size you choose, you may clip a newsprint pad to an easel or lay it flat on a table top.
- You can also use individual sheets of newsprint, either clipped to an easel or laid flat on a table top.

Reference Tools

- Children's thesaurus
- Children's dictionary

Writing Tools (organized in bins or tubbies)

- Crayons, markers, pencils, pens
- Rubber stamps, stickers
- Assorted paper
  - ~ Grade-level lined and unlined
  - ~ Construction paper (9- x 12-inch, 12- x 18-inch, and scraps)
  - ~ Scrapbooking paper (8.5 x 11-inch)
  - ~ Patterned paper
  - ~ Novelty papers in a variety of themes
- Manila file folders
- Correction tape

Publishing Tools (organized in bins or tubbies)

- Glue, glue sticks, tape
- Scissors, stapler, hole punch, yarn scraps
- Construction paper or scrapbooking paper

- Assorted pictures for projects and activities
    - ~ Old magazines, calendars, toy catalogs to cut and paste
        - If you don't subscribe to magazines, ask friends and family. Or, you can often get them free or nearly free at your local public library.
        - Save the toy ads from the Sunday newspaper.
        - Visit a dollar store for very inexpensive calendars.
    - ~ Images from the Internet to print, cut, and paste
        - Royalty-free images
            - Flickr: **www.flickr.com/creativecommons**
            - FreeFoto: **www.freefoto.com**
            - Stock.Xchng: **www.sxc.hu**
            - Free Clip Art: **www.clip-art.com**
        - Google image search
            1. Visit **www.google.com** and click "Images."
            2. Practice Internet safety. Click "Advanced Image Search" and choose "Use strict filtering."
            3. Type in your search term (bee, train, rainbow, etc.) and click "Search Images."
            4. A page of photos will appear. Scroll through till you find one that will be suitable for your needs.

Optional

- **Floor or Tabletop Easel** (see p. 10)
- **Pocket Chart** (see pp. 10-11)

Additional Lesson-Specific Supplies

Lesson 1

- Paper streamers (crêpe-paper party streamers or strips of tissue paper)
- Yarn scraps

Lesson 2

- Five 12- x 18-inch sheets of construction paper in light colors such as white, yellow, or powder blue
- 10-inch paper plate
- Bits of yarn or fabric
- Optional
    - ~ Digital camera
    - ~ Nonfiction book or magazine article about animals
    - ~ Children's encyclopedia software

Lesson 3

- Several pictures from magazines or old calendars depicting different kinds of weather
- Craft sticks
- Small file box with blank 3- x 5-inch index cards

- Yarn
- Spring-type clothespins or paper clips

Lesson 4

- Brown construction paper
- Children's dictionary and thesaurus
- Cookie jar or other container that works as a substitute
- Batch of cookies (either homemade or store-bought)
- Optional
  - ~ Card-making software program

Lesson 5

- Picture of a train
- Optional
  - ~ Construction or scrapbooking paper in gold or yellow
  - ~ Small self-closing baggies

Lesson 6

- Pointers, or materials to make them (see p. 89, Advance Prep)
- Small (1/4- or 1/2-inch) round stickers (either solid color or with a fun decoration)
- Star-shaped stickers (1/4- or 1/2-inch)
- Picture of a rainbow
- Dinner-sized white paper plate
- Cardboard, poster board, or tagboard
- Optional
  - ~ Paintings of a famous artist from a book, Internet, or art collection. (If you decide to visit an art museum for this activity, be sure to stop at the gift shop. Help your child choose a postcard of a favorite painting to bring home.)

Lesson 7

- Pointers
- Small round stickers (1/4- or 1/2-inch)
- Star-shaped stickers (1/4- or 1/2-inch)
- Construction or scrapbooking paper in a variety of solid colors, including green
- Three-ring binder
- Optional
  - ~ Paper dinner plate divided into three sections
  - ~ Paper bowls
  - ~ Small paper cup
  - ~ Plastic knife, fork, and spoon
  - ~ Construction or scrapbooking paper in a variety of colors including green, brown, and white
  - ~ Card-making software program

Lesson 8

- *My Garden of Rhyming Words* notebook from Activity Set 7:2
- Construction or scrapbooking paper in a variety of solid colors, including green
- Cardboard milk carton
- Old sheer nylon stocking
- Optional butterfly net and magnifying glass
- *Story Idea Box* from Activity Set 3:3
- Lightweight 10-inch paper plates
- Yarn
- Optional
    - ~ Large sheets of butcher paper in a light color
    - ~ Tissue paper or shredded newspaper

Lesson 9

- *My Garden of Rhyming Words* notebook from Activity Set 7:2
- *Story Idea Box* from Activity Set 3:3
- Yellow construction or scrapbooking paper
- White butcher paper (or gift wrap with one plain white side)
- Optional
    - ~ Encyclopedia article, website, or science book about ladybugs
    - ~ 10-inch white paper plate
    - ~ Red construction paper
    - ~ Black crayon or marker
    - ~ Metal paper fasteners or brads
    - ~ Digital camera
    - ~ Props to perform a simple play

Lesson 10

- *My Garden of Rhyming Words* notebook from Activity Set 7:2
- Construction or scrapbooking paper in a variety of solid colors, including green
- Butcher paper or a solid-color sheet of gift wrap
- 9- x 12-inch construction paper in black
- White chalk or crayon
- Toy car
- Optional
    - ~ 12- x 18-inch construction paper in pink and green
    - ~ Blank index cards
    - ~ Watermelon seeds and planting materials

Picture Book Suggestions

We know you will want to take care in choosing just the right picture book for each lesson. There are so many wonderful read-alouds with delightful story lines and engaging illustrations. Start with your own bookshelves—they may already hold all the books you'll need for the lessons in WriteShop Primary Book A.

If not, with a little advance planning you'll have time to scour used book stores, yard sales, and the library in your search for the "perfect" book. For guidance, ask your local children's librarian, read book reviews online, or seek out the recommendation of friends. We've also put together a list of books your family might enjoy during your WriteShop Primary adventure.

Though we have taken care to select titles that are artistically pleasing and wholesome in content, *we make no guarantee that our recommendations will always match your family's criteria for acceptable reading.* So the final decision, of course, is yours. Some of these titles are timeless enough to appeal to all ages. Others may suit your five-year-old but not your seven-year-old. These are merely suggestions to help you think about enjoyable titles that will fit with each lesson. Please use this list as a springboard rather than the final word.

Lesson 1: Picture book about one kind of animal

- *Millions of Cats* by Wanda Gág
- *The Mitten* by Jan Brett
- *Five O' Clock Charlie* by Marguerite Henry
- *Fritz and the Beautiful Horses* by Jan Brett
- *The Whales* by Cynthia Rylant

Lesson 2: Picture book or easy reader about a famous person

- *The Glorious Flight* by Alice and Martin Provensen
- *Fannie in the Kitchen: The Whole Story from Soup to Nuts of How Fannie Farmer Invented Recipes with Precise Measurements* by Deborah Hopkinson
- *Gregor Mendel: The Friar Who Grew Peas* by Cheryl Bardoe
- *Ruth Law Thrills a Nation* by Don Brown
- *Snowflake Bentley* by Jacqueline Briggs Martin
- *A Weed Is a Flower: The Life of George Washington Carver* by Aliki

Lesson 3: Picture book about something the child likes to think about or do

Book choice will be more personal, depending on the child's interests. Consider books with subjects most kids enjoy, such as the beach, soccer, special time with Dad, fire trucks, dolls, the moon, flying, or chocolate!

- *Just Me and My Dad* by Mercer Mayer
- *Just Grandma and Me* by Mercer Mayer
- *Lentil* by Robert McCloskey
- *Flicka, Ricka, Dicka Bake a Cake* by Maj Lindman
- *In the Woods: Who's Been Here?* by Lindsay Barrett George

Lesson 4: Picture book about friends

- *Hondo and Fabian* by Peter McCarty
- *Frog and Toad are Friends* by Arnold Lobel
- *Best Friends for Frances* by Russell Hoban
- *Flicka, Ricka, Dicka and Their New Friend* by Maj Lindman
- *Where Are You Going? To See My Friend!* by Eric Carle and Kazuo Iwamura
- *Mrs. Katz and Tush* by Patricia Polacco
- *Thy Friend, Obadiah* by Brinton Turkle

Lesson 5: Picture book about trains

- *The Little Engine That Could* by Watty Piper
- *Smokey* by Bill Peet
- *Two Little Trains* by Margaret Wise Brown
- *Little Train* by Lois Lenski

Lesson 6: Picture book or easy reader about colors

Make sure text is written in complete sentences, not just individual words.

Scientific book that explains colors

- *The Magic School Bus Makes a Rainbow: A Book about Color* by Joanna Cole

Or picture book that describes colored objects

- *A Color of His Own* by Leo Lionni
- *Lemons Are Not Red* by Laura Vaccaro Seeger
- *Brown Bear, Brown Bear, What Do You See?* by Bill Martin and Eric Carle
- *My Many Colored Days* by Dr. Seuss
- *Babar's Book of Color* by Laurent de Brunhoff
- *The Deep Blue Sea: A Book of Colors* by Audrey Wood

Lesson 7: Picture book with rhyming text

Picture book written in verse

- *Green Eggs and Ham, Horton Hatches the Egg,* and other books by Dr. Seuss
- *The Owl and the Pussycat* by Edward Lear and Jan Brett
- *Over In the Meadow* by Olive A. Wadsworth
- *Gold Fever* and *Covered Wagons, Bumpy Trails* by Verla Kay
- *Is Your Mama a Llama?* by Steven Kellogg
- *King Bidgood's in the Bathtub* by Audrey Wood
- *Jesse Bear, What Will You Wear?* by Nancy White Carlstrom
- *D is for Drinking Gourd: An African-American Alphabet* by Nancy I. Sanders

Or book of children's poems

- *Random House Book of Poetry for Children* compiled by Jack Prelutsky
- *Favorite Poems Old and New* by Helen Ferris Tibbets
- *A Child's Garden of Verses* by Robert Louis Stevenson

Lesson 8: Nonfiction picture book about insects or spiders

- *Ant Cities* by Arthur Dorros
- *Are You a Grasshopper?* By Judy Allen and Tudor Humphries
- *Spiders (My First Look at: Insects)* by Theresa Wimmer
- *Ladybugs* by Claire Llewellyn
- *The Beetle Alphabet Book* by Jerry Pallotta

Lesson 9: Picture book about the personal experience of a child who is about the same age as yours

- *Blueberries for Sal* and *One Morning in Maine* by Robert McCloskey
- *My Mother Is the Most Beautiful Woman in the World: A Russian Folktale* by Becky Rayher
- *When I Was Young in the Mountains* by Cynthia Rylant
- *All Those Secrets of the World* by Jane Yolen
- *Keep the Lights Burning, Abbie* by Peter Roop
- *All the Places to Love* by Patricia MacLachlan
- *My Great Aunt Arizona* by Gloria Houston
- *Where the Wild Things Are* by Maurice Sendak

Lesson 10: Picture storybook about a vehicle such as a dump truck, a school bus, or a race car

- *Mike Mulligan's Steam Shovel* by Virginia Lee Burton
- *The Berenstain Bears and the Big Road Race* by Stan and Jan Berenstain
- *Katy and the Big Snow* by Virginia Lee Burton
- *Little Toot* by Hardie Gramatsky

Index